Why People Are Praising Toie Martin and *Living Your Life With Possibilities*

"*Living Your Life With Possibilities* is jam-packed with inspiration and practical steps to take your life to the next level. As Toie Martin states, 'You are the most important organization you will ever work for,' so you owe it to yourself to read this book and discover how you can improve your life multifold. Every page will lead you one step closer to the happiness you seek."

— Tyler R. Tichelaar, PhD and award-winning author of *Narrow Lives* and *The Best Place*

"Toie Martin has mastered what it means to create your own destiny. Refusing to be held back by the resistance so many of us feel, she created a life of possibilities for herself, and now in these pages, she shares that process with others. The result is a thoughtful, inspiring, practical, and purposeful journey for anyone who wants more from life and is willing to get out of their own way to achieve it."

— Patrick Snow, Publishing Coach and Best-Selling Author of *Creating Your Own Destiny* and *Boy Entrepreneur*

"*Living Your Life With Possibilities* is one of those books you want to share with the people in your life. It's inspiring, funny, and an absolute must. This how-to guide will help you navigate your life with courage, confidence, and grace."

— Jeri Glassner, BS Social Work, MBA in International Management, Senior Operations Administrator

"Toie Martin's approach to understanding change, achieving success, and creating the habits we really want is a truly innovative way for organizations and individuals to approach the way we create what comes next in our lives and where we work."

— Brandy Buffington, BS Cardiopulmonary Care,
Hospital Sales Specialist

"This book is a game-changer for anyone who wants to live their life to the fullest. There are many books out there that give advice, but *Living Your Life With Possibilities* takes it to the next level. It will inspire you through stories and give you easy tools to start creating the habits and life you really want."

— Amy Scott, BA Psychology, M.Ed Counseling and Human
Resources, Professional Relations Liaison

"This book has lessons for kids and adults that will plant the seeds of Social Emotional Learning, which will, in turn, inspire the habits that create the life skills we need to be successful in our relationships, careers, and lives. I highly recommend it and give it an A+!"

— Lisa Barbour, BS, M.Ed School
Administration, School Counseling

"This is a great story of true grit, real determination, and the quest for understanding what true happiness is and how to achieve it. You will love each and every lesson."

— Debbie Vickery,
Resource Support Specialist

"In *Living Your Life With Possibilities,* Toie Martin shares hard-earned truths about life, the limitations the world tries to enforce upon us, and the possibilities that exist for success, happiness, and joy when we refuse to be limited. Grab this book and experience the wonderful life awaiting you."

— Nicole Gabriel, Author of *Finding Your Inner Truth* and *Stepping Into Your Becoming*

"With expert guidance, the author gently takes you by the hand to share invaluable practical advice for getting unstuck. Her powerful five-step formula helps you to break out of your comfort zone, enabling you to discover and create new possibilities to live life fearlessly whatever your circumstances."

— Susan Friedmann, CSP, and International Best-Selling Author of *Riches in Niches: How to Make it BIG in a small market*

LIVING YOUR LIFE WITH POSSIBILITIES

5 PRACTICAL STEPS TO LEADING YOURSELF AND OTHERS WITH CONFIDENCE, COURAGE, AND GRACE

TOIE MARTIN

AVIVA PUBLISHING
New York

Living Your Life With Possibilities:
Five Practical Steps to Leading Yourself and Others With Confidence, Courage, and Grace

Published by:
Aviva Publishing
Lake Placid, NY
(518) 523-1320
www.AvivaPubs.com

Toie Martin
806-881-6331
ToieMartin@InnovativeFundamentals.com
ToieMartin.com
LivingYourLifeWithPossibilities.com

ISBN: 9781950241033
Library of Congress: 2019904340

Editors: Tyler Tichelaar and Larry Alexander, Superior Book Productions
Cover Design and Interior Book Layout: Nicole Gabriel, Angel Dog Productions

Every attempt has been made to source properly all quotes.
Printed in the United States of America
First Edition

For Mom and Dad, who showed me
how to live with possibilities.

For my son Tag,
who believed in me even when I didn't believe in myself.
You have the kindest heart and inspire me daily.

For my amazing friends,
you are my family, and my life would not be as bright without you.

I love you all with all my heart.

“The jump is so frightening
between where I am,
And where I want to be…
Because of all I may become,
I will close my eyes and leap!”

— Mary Anne Radmacher

ACKNOWLEDGMENTS

So many amazing thought leaders have influenced my journey through their research and passionate work to help create a more compassionate, kind, and educated world for us to live in. I would like to thank in particular:

Shawn Achor, Maya Angelou, Brené Brown, Paulo Coelho, Ellen DeGeneres, Bill George, Elizabeth Gilbert, Daniel Goleman, TD Jakes, Michael Pollen, Jen Sincero, Simon Sinek, Cheryl Strayed, and last but certainly not least, Oprah Winfrey.

Thank you to all of my friends and family who have supported me in this long and sometimes painful journey. Your love, support, and laughter make the world a better place.

I would also like to thank Patrick Snow, Tyler Tichelaar, Larry Alexander, and Nicole Gabriel. Without them, this book would still be an incomplete document on my laptop.

CONTENT

Introduction: Creating the Change I Want to See 19

PART I: EMBRACING CHANGE **25**

Chapter One: Changing...with Confidence, Courage, and Grace **27**

The Right Change
Understanding Change Management
It's as Easy as 1, 2, 3, 4, 5
What Changes?
Self-Confidence and Change
Seeing the Change before Others
Changing the Change Curve
Know Better, Change Better
Hardwiring Habits
Change Education
The Changing Brain
How Well Do We Score at Change?
Exercises

Chapter 2: Thriving to Reach Endless Possibilities **51**

Connecting Our Two Brains
The Four Domains of Emotional Intelligence
Are We Becoming Less Civilized?
Thrive On
Innovative Fundamentals: Seven Areas of Life
Innovative Fundamentals Seven Area Man (SAM)
Pneumonic for Seven Area Man (SAM)
Exercises

Chapter 3: Connecting...with Yourself and Others **73**

Connectedness
Seeing New Connections

Connecting with Yourself
Connecting with Others
Connecting with the Work We Do
Learning through Our Experiences
Innovative Fundamentals Map Approach
Connecting What You Already Know
Connecting Our Thoughts and Actions
Exercises

Chapter 4: Leading…Yourself and Others **89**

You, Inc.
Derailing
Learning to Lead Yourself
Lemonade Stand or Fortune 500
You Are the Most Important Organization You Will Ever Work For
Establishing a Clear Purpose
Selecting Board Members
Exercises

PART II: SELF-AWARENESS **107**

Chapter 5: Knowing Who You Are and What You Stand For **109**

Know Thyself
What Do I See?
Prepare for a Hijacking
Self-Awareness Skills
Connecting Self-Awareness Skills to the Change Process
Creating New Awareness
Tuning into Our Internal GPS
Tools for Developing Self-Awareness Skills
Exercises

Chapter 6: Seeing…the Possibilities 125

Lemons to Lemonade to Lemonade Stand
Seeing the Glass Half Full
Seeing with an Open Mind
Seeing Our Habits—the Good, the Bad, and the Ugly
Problems and Possibilities
Why, Baby, Why?
Step 1: Define the Problem/See the Possibilities
Tools for Defining Problems and Seeing Possibilities
Exercises

Chapter 7: Measuring…Where Am I Now? 141

The Chicken or the Egg?
What Gets Measured Improves
Be Careful What You Measure (Wish) For
I Am Here
I'm a 10
Step 2: Where Am I/Where Are We?
Tools for Developing Self-Awareness Skills
Exercises

Chapter 8: Focusing on What You Want 155

Keeping Your Eye on the Prize
The Lost Art of Focus
You Have to Make a Goal to Score
Creating AHA moments
Step 3: Where Do I Want to Be/Where Do We Want to Be?
Exercises

PART III: SELF-MANAGEMENT 165

Chapter 9: Managing Yourself with Confidence, Courage, and Grace 167

Fear…the Other F Word

Going Pro
Self-Management Skills
Exercises

Chapter 10: Getting There 177

Are We There Yet?
Going Places
Leading Our Actions
PDSA: Plan, Do, Study, Act
Step 4: How Do I/We Get There?
Exercises

Chapter 11: Maintaining Success 187

You Are Not Alone
Oh, I Can't Decide
Staying Hungry
Show Me Who Your Friends Are
A Little Gratitude Goes a Long Way
Step 5: How Do I/We Stay Here?
Exercises

PART IV: SOCIAL AWARENESS 199

Chapter 12: Empathizing with and Understanding Others 215

I Feel Ya
It's My Pleasure
Who's Wearing the Pants Here?
Seeing Possibilities Where Others See Limitations
Social Awareness Skills
Social Awareness Skills and Change
Exercises

PART V: RELATIONSHIP MANAGEMENT 227

Chapter 13: Managing Relationships 215

Managing Your Relationships
Trust: The Seed of a Good Relationship
Value Yourself, Value Your Relationships
Now You're Speaking My Language
There Is No I in Team
Relationship Management Skills
Relationship Management Skills and Change
Exercises

PART VI: INNOVATIVE FUNDAMENTALS APPROACH 225

Chapter 14: Building a Thriving Organizational Culture 227

Leader…It's More Than a Title
Thriving People Create Thriving Organizations
Why Choose "Or" When You Can Choose "And"?
Benefitting From Personal Growth in a Professional Setting
Who Made That Decision?
The Power of Inclusion
Exercises

Chapter 15: Creating Schools Where Students and Staff Thrive 241

Possibilities in the Classroom
Understanding Ourselves and Others
What Can an SEL Program Achieve in Your School?
Exercises

A Final Note 249
Appendix Tools 251
About the Author 263
About Coaching, Classes, and Workshops 265
Book Toie Martin to Speak 267

"Your attitude to life is probably the crucial starting place, the most important ingredient that will determine what you make of it. I say "be positive." And by that, I mean be highly active and enthusiastic. Do things! Engage with life; don't drift across the surface. Initiate things. Get involved and take on plenty—plenty of responsibilities and projects, plenty of opportunities and adventures. If we don't improve, we don't grow. If we don't grow, are we really alive?"

— Author Unknown

INTRODUCTION

CREATING THE CHANGE I WANT TO SEE

"Those who dare to fail miserably can achieve greatly."

— John F. Kennedy

I had been a registered nurse for ten years, had just turned forty, and was working for my first horrible boss (unfortunately, not my last) when my dear friend smacked me right upside the face with the question, "What do you dream about accomplishing? What would your perfect life look like?" I felt like he was speaking a foreign language. I was trying to maintain my calm, cool, and collected exterior, but I was freaking out on the inside and probably looked like I had just seen a three-headed, purple alien walk through my living room with a peanut butter and jelly sandwich. I was a single mom with two precious boys, two jobs, and a deadbeat ex-husband. My dream was to have enough time and energy to take a bath alone at the end of the day after we watched *Scooby Doo* rather than *Barney* again, to be able to pay all my bills at the end of the month, and to fit into the jeans I had just bought on sale that were too small but such a good deal. I didn't have any idea what I wanted to accomplish or what I wanted my life to look like. I had been too busy surviving even to think about it.

Call it a midlife crisis, an epiphany, a mental breakdown, a wakeup call, a walk about, or a come-to-Jesus meeting.... Whatever it was, I knew one door was closing and another opening. I didn't know what the door looked like or where it was, but I knew it was out there, and that it was important. The fear of entering the unknown was suddenly less significant than working in an environment that, at times, felt like a combat zone, and other times, a school playground where bullies push you around, steal your lunch money, and make fun of your jacked-up teeth or wrong-sized thighs. As I laid my resignation on my boss's desk, I felt as liberated and free as Andy Dufrane in *The Shawshank Redemption* after he crawled through several feet of sewage pipe to his freedom. I could practically feel the rain falling out of the sky onto my bare chest as I raised my arms to the heavens. But this feeling was quickly followed by "Oh, crap, what have I done? Did I really just resign from the best-paying job I have ever had?"

Over the next two years, I would earn my MBA, get certified in Lean Six Sigma, and start my new career in process improvement, project management, and large change management projects. While leading multi-million-dollar change projects at work, my largest change projects were unfolding in my personal life. During this time, I discovered a common formula for all change—one practical, five-step formula for all change based on two sets of skills.

The bad news is most of us never get any formal learning on change or the two skill sets required to create it successfully. When you think about it, it really sounds kind of crazy that change is so important and continual in our lives, yet we don't really get the opportunity to learn how to create it. The good news is we can change that, and it's not hard.

To me, living your life with possibilities means feeling confident about who you are and what's important to you; having the courage to push yourself out of your comfort zone to learn, grow, and experience new things; and leading yourself and others with grace to promote an environment where creativity, innovation, and growth can thrive. Achieving all of these goals requires some kind of change, yet most of us never get any formal or informal education on change. Our schools and jobs are measuring how well we add, subtract, read, and work, but not how well we are thriving.

This book is for people who want to feel confident and courageous about creating what comes next in their personal lives or organizations, and who want a practical way to do it.

Here's how this book works…

Part I has four chapters on changing, thriving, connecting, and leading. These chapters all talk about change. You'll learn how change really works, from creating an idea in our heads to completion; why change is really important; how innovative research on thriving reveals the skills we need to make change happen effectively; how to connect to ourselves and the people and things we value; and why we must practice authentic leadership of ourselves before we can be authentic leaders of others.

Then Chapters 5 to 13 are separated into four key parts, one for each of the four domains of Emotional Intelligence: Part II: Self-Awareness, Part III: Self-Management, Part IV: Social Awareness, And Part V: Relationship Management. Most chapters have activities at the end so you can start applying the skills from that chapter. Remember practice makes habits.

Finally, Part VI talks about how the Innovative Fundamentals approach can be used in organizations and school systems to promote a culture of continual growth, respect for ourselves and others, team work, collaboration, and leadership. This approach can promote a complete K-12 Social and Emotional Learning program that will prepare the next generation to be leaders of change in the workforce and their personal lives and allow organizations to educate and include all staff in creating successful change in their work areas and their lives so they can perform at their best and achieve what they are capable of achieving.

I hope you enjoy discovering how the Innovative Fundamentals Approach can help you find and live your purpose with courage, confidence, and grace, whether that is by opening your own business, loving the work you are already doing, raising your children with love and compassion, painting the perfect picture, creating better relationships with friends, finding the love of your life, or growing the perfect pecan tree.

Here's to your success in all your endeavors!

Toie Martin

"The biggest adventure you can take is to live the life of your dreams."

— Oprah Winfrey

PART I
EMBRACING CHANGE

CHAPTER ONE

CHANGING...WITH CONFIDENCE, COURAGE, AND GRACE

"The world as we created it is a process of our thinking. It cannot be changed without changing our thinking."

— Albert Einstein

THE RIGHT CHANGE

You don't have to go very far to see examples of people who seem to be living a better life than you, making more money, going on more vacations, and even seeming to have better-looking friends. You also don't have to look very far to find a large number of things you can buy so you, too, can have a wonderful life. You can swipe your card through the machine, take your new toys home, start using them, and get ready for your life to change. The birds will sing louder, the sun will shine brighter, your hair will grow evenly, potholes will repair themselves, those jeans you got on sale for a ridiculously low price will now fit...

and your life will be significantly better. Just swipe your card, and wait for the transformation to begin.

Wait for it.....

The truth is, we have a plethora of opportunities to choose from every day. In fact, we have more opportunities at our fingertips than any generation before us. How do we pick from these opportunities? How do we choose what and who we want to spend our time, money, and energy on? How do we sift through and separate the opportunities from the distractions? How do we decide what opportunities are right for us so we don't waste time seeking something we have had all along or even worse, something we didn't even really want in the first place? What do you value? Whom do you value? What brings you the most joy? What makes you sad? What makes you want to jump out of your chair ready for a fight? What scares you? What are you dreaming about achieving? These questions help us to grow in the right direction. Growth is change and change is part of being alive.

Change is a significant part of life—so significant, in fact, that change is actually one of life's defining characteristics.

According to Oxford Dictionaries, "Life" is "The condition that distinguishes animals and plants from organic matter, including the capacity for growth, reproduction, functional activity, and **continual change preceding death**."

Continual change preceding death! Yeah, change is kind of a really big deal!

I'm not sure what your beliefs are around mindfulness, meditation, prayer, self-awareness, gratitude, and related practices. I can tell you that I have always been a believer, although I was generally much too busy and distracted running in all directions to stop, be still, meditate, and realize I was going a lot of places and nowhere at the same time, like a hamster on an exercise wheel. A very tired hamster! I'm telling you this now because these simple acts are an important part of the change process, and more importantly, they are part of the skill set we need to help us with the first three steps of creating successful change. They are how we connect to our inner thoughts.

You know, that gut instinct that gives us a little tingle when things feel right and an uneasy feeling when things don't? This is the connection we create between our thoughts and actions, or our mind and soul. The more in tune we are with our feelings and emotions, the louder and clearer our gut instinct is. It is our internal GPS system. Let's say we are going on a long trip. Let's call it "life." Our GPS needs to know where we are right now and where we want to go so it can analyze the routes for getting you there. Along your trip, you look at your GPS to make sure you are still on the right path. Our internal GPS relies on our self-awareness skills to understand where we are and where we want to go in the future. We develop self-awareness by practicing mindful activities on a regular basis like meditation, prayer, drawing, walking in nature, painting, fishing, planting, and yoga (hot, cold, with goats, with babies, or just plain). Basically, a mindful activity is any activity where we focus on one thing and get our minds into a state of relaxation. It is the exact opposite of multitasking.

We are bombarded by thousands of pieces of information every second—so much information that we can't even begin to make sense of it as it's happening. It's during moments of mindfulness and reflection that we can look back and make sense of all of the information—all that has happened in our day and our world. Not practicing mindfulness is like setting your GPS for a really important, long trip (life), and then only checking it occasionally (or never) to see if you are still going in the right direction.

Take a deep breath, relax, and think about this….

The words below are a simple way to explain change management. They have been attributed to Ralph Waldo Emerson, Lao Tzu, Frank Outlaw, Gautama Buddha, Bishop Mark Beckwith, and even Margaret Thatcher's father. We can't be sure who wrote them, but we do know that slightly different versions of this chain of words have been around since the 1800s. Since the 1800s! So, long before the technology existed to see inside the brain to study how it works and long before there were shelves full of books on change, there was some understanding that our thoughts are at the core of our actions and our destiny.

> Watch your *thoughts*, for they become *words*.
> Watch your *words*, for they become *actions*.
> Watch your *actions*, for they become *habits*.
> Watch your *habits*, for they become your *character*.
> And watch your *character*, for it becomes your *destiny*.
> What we think, we become.

UNDERSTANDING CHANGE MANAGEMENT

Many of you may think Change Management is the department that keeps making all of the changes in your work area. Actually, it is the coordination of a transition from Situation A to Situation B in order to achieve lasting change. It involves managing the change in processes along with the people-side of the change process. For example, if you decide that a vegan diet is the way you want to cook for you and your family's health, you must change many of the processes you currently use to prepare meals. This is managing the process part of change. The people-side of change involves the family members changing their thoughts and habits around their diet and getting on board with new Vegan habits instead. It is the act of connecting our thoughts, words, actions, and behaviors to achieve the outcomes we want. It involves emotional intelligence skills to help us manage our thoughts and feelings so we can create the actions and behavors and, ultimately, the change we want. Successful change management includes people and processes changing together.

Think about it like this.... If you took your car apart and laid it out on your front lawn, you would have perfectly good parts, but they would not take you where you wanted to go unless they were all put back together correctly. I find change management to be much the same. The ability to change, adapt, and grow is vital to our success, and if we are trying to use the parts lying out on the lawn as our tool, we are not going to get where we want to be. On the other hand, if all the parts are put together to create a car, it will take us wherever we want to go.

Close your eyes and picture this.... Change Management (CM) is your vehicle. It is your tool for getting you where you want to go. Your thoughts and your actions are just parts until they combine to create your vehicle.

IT'S AS EASY AS 1, 2, 3, 4, 5

When I was a college student, I was very lucky to have my own apartment. I did have to work full time to afford it, which meant I was poor and busy. I had a few different dishes I liked to eat and knew how to cook, and by that, I mean four different types of casserole. Each Sunday and Wednesday, I would prepare a large casserole and then eat it for lunch and supper practically every day until it was gone. The ease of getting to cook once for several meals allowed me to focus my time and energy on school and work. Time management at its finest. I can't tell you how many of those five-ingredient recipe paperback cookbooks I have bought while waiting in the grocery store line, and have never used. There's no way I could ever cook all of the recipes in the books

I already own, but there is something so alluring about the simplicity of five simple ingredients that I just can't pass up. I'm telling you this because the development of Emotional Intelligence and the powerful programs organizations use for Process Improvement and Project Management all require the same five steps. Yep, the same five fundamental steps for creating change. Which really does make sense given that our thoughts and actions are connected to each other.

5 STEPS FOR DEVELOPING EMOTIONAL INTELLIGENCE	5 STEPS FOR IMPROVING PROCESSES (ACTIONS)
1. Define the behavior you want to change.	1.Define the problem/opportunity
2. Measure the behavior you want to change	2. Measure current state
3. Identify new desired behavior	3. Analyze future state
4. Implement new behavior	4. Implement changes
5. Sustain new behavior	5. Maintain improvements

WHAT CHANGES?

It's actually much easier to answer what doesn't change. The answer: Nothing. Every hour, every minute, every second of every day, we and everything around us is changing. Change is part of being alive. The trees, the plants, the flowers, the grass, the animals (wild and domestic), and humans...we are all in a constant state of change. Living on Earth, which is also in a constant state of change, and working in an era defined by massive changes shaping the business climate, we see change everywhere. It is constant.

Whether you realize it or not, no matter how old or young you are, change is a big part of your life, and it is highly unlikely you were formally trained to manage change. Change comes in many different forms, and it's like an emotion—you don't always know when it is coming or what it will look like, but you do get to choose what to do with it. How well you manage change will affect the quality of your life and the lives of those around you.

If you are reading this, I can assume you are alive, and if you are alive, you are changing. All living things are constantly growing and changing. . .even your aunt Betty who has worn the same purple pants and pink sweater as long as you can remember—are changing. We change because we want to, we change because we have to, and sometimes we change without even realizing we've changed at all as experiences shape our lives and our beliefs.

When we are born, we are equipped with a few basic survival skills. As we grow, we learn from our environment. We weren't born knowing how to manage money, how to dress, or even whether to put mustard or ketchup on our hot dogs—we learn from our parents and our environment. These experiences form the habits of our lives. Only when we mature do we start to look around and see other ways to do things. Our habits are the culmination of what we learned from our parents, friends, TV, social media, etc. Once we are grown, these habits continue to be shaped by our environment and experiences and become our own, adult habits.

Like many of you, I have had more than a few moments when change has come barrelling into my life uninvited and unexpected. We can prepare for many things. . .if we have a game or recital coming up, we practice. If we have an interview or test, we practice. If we are speaking in public or trying to create the perfect lasagna, we practice. So why don't we practice our change management skills? Our quality of life greatly depends on our ability to create and manage change, but we rarely have the skills and certainly haven't practiced them. What would happen if we knew the steps of change management and practiced them as part of our daily lives? What would happen if our children saw this and learned to create these habits from a young age? What if we changed the change curve!

SELF-CONFIDENCE AND CHANGE

In one of my all-time favorite movies, *How to Train Your Dragon* by DreamWorks Animation, Hiccup is a young boy who lives in a beautiful village perched on the side of magnificent cliffs. The sunsets are breathtaking, the meadows are lush, and if not for the large flying dragons, life would be pretty peaceful. Fighting the dragons is everything in the village. The children are taught to become Vikings and attend Dragon School where they learn to slay dragons, but Hiccup is not like the other children in the village. He doesn't have their athletic skills or killer instincts, and he feels uncomfortable with the whole thought of fighting and killing. One day, he asks his father, "Has anyone ever tried to train a dragon?" His father replies, "No one has ever lived to tell about it." So, while the entire village is trying to make more and better tools to fight the dragons, Hiccup is off trying to understand "Toothless," the dragon he shot out of the sky with a flying net he built. Hiccup originally intends to find Toothless and kill him, but instead, he cuts him loose. However, Toothless is injured from Hiccup's net and cannot fly. Hiccup continues to visit Toothless and even provides him with food while he is unable to hunt. The two begin to understand each other and work together. Eventually, they show the rest of the village they don't have to fight, but instead, can work together to fight the queen dragon and stop the dragons from attacking the village. By the end of the movie, the people of the village and the dragons are working together to build a better community, rather than endlessly rebuilding the destruction caused from battling the dragons.

The Vikings in Hiccup's village would have continued to fight those dragons if one courageous boy hadn't looked for a different way of doing things. Once the Vikings and the dragons realize they really want the same things, they work together. The energy wasted on constantly rebuilding and repairing is turned into continual improvement and growth. Hiccup was self-aware enough to know he would feel terrible if he killed Toothless, and he was confident that he was smart enough to find a solution through understanding the dragons first.

It takes courage and self-confidence to be the change you want to see. It's easy instead to think, *Who am I to think I can make a difference? Who am I to speak up? Who am I to suggest a different way?* Yeah, you're right; we all have a hundred different stories we can tell ourselves to sabotage our goals and dreams. Our desire to stay safe and comfortable creates fear and self-doubt about our ability to reach the next level. We all have fears and self-doubts! My favorite stories to tell myself are "I am not smart enough," "I'm not pretty enough," "I don't know enough"—all with an undertone of "I'm not worthy." However, I choose not to believe any of my old stories. I am no less afraid than I was a year ago, or two years ago, or even three...but I am moving forward and sharing despite my fears. I am doing that in hopes that this method helps you and me to be the best versions of ourselves so we can achieve the success we desire.

SEEING THE CHANGE BEFORE OTHERS

Oprah Winfrey has spent years in the spotlight talking about her journey of overcoming her self-doubt and the naysayers to become one of the most successful and influential people in the world. She talks about how excited she was to have a job as a news anchor. However, the excitement eventually diminished. Because it was thought to be a glamorous, sought-after position, she stayed at it longer than she wanted. Her heart wasn't in it, and her bosses at the TV station where she worked knew it. They were trying to get her to quit when they demoted her to doing a local talk show to finish out her contract.

Oprah talks about her and her best friend Gayle were sitting over a glass of wine, ecstatic that she was twenty-two years old and making

$22,000 a year. Oprah's goal was to make her age, so she set a new goal of making $40,000 a year by the time she was forty. To do that, she knew she would need to find another job. However, her dad was in her ear telling her she would never find another job as good, so she better hang on to it—"Who is going to pay you more money than you are making now?" she heard him say.

Oprah kept her position at the TV station for a while, but she knew it was a job and not a calling. When she began hosting the talk show, she knew she was closer to her calling. If Oprah had listened to others and her own self-doubt about not being good enough, she wouldn't be the Oprah we know and love today. Millions of people around the world would have missed out on the knowledge and wisdom she has shared through her remarkable approach to life and learning to live with purpose. She persevered when others gave up. She created a platform where one didn't exist. She tuned into her gut and relentlessly focused on creating a show where thought leaders had a platform to inspire and share their knowledge and experiences. She became the change she wanted to see. Are you the change you want to see?

We can learn to be fierce self-leaders of ourselves, our lives, our homes, and our beliefs…and we can bring our skills with us to school, work, the field, the court, the boardroom, the Sunday school class, the Senate, the House, and everywhere in between. We can be a part of creating self-confidence, self-awareness, and self-respect so we can have confidence, awareness, and respect for others. We can be the change we want to see in ourselves, our families, our organizations, our communities, our schools, our states, our countries, and our world.

CHANGING THE CHANGE CURVE

Almost fifty years ago, 1969 to be exact, Elisabeth Kübler-Ross created the Grief Model (see below) to help identify the stages of grief people go through when faced with a terminal illness or the loss of someone close to them. The model is so well known it has been mentioned in movies like *Dead Pool II* and *Madea's Family Funeral.* Kübler-Ross, a Swiss-American psychologist who pioneered work in the areas of death, dying, and the grieving process, began to study grief to identify the different stages people go through when dealing with the most permanent form of change there is...death. She presents the five stages; denial, anger, bargaining, depression, and acceptance, in a graph to show the general order people go through the stages. Kübler-Ross found that everyone going through grief didn't go through these steps in exactly the same order; in fact, some people skipped over stages entirely while others got stuck for years before moving on. I first learned about this model from the staff at Hospice where my dad was a patient for the last three months of his life, then again in psychology class in college, and again in nursing school when we studied end-of-life issues.

Elisabeth Kubler-Ross Grief Model (1969)/ Change Curve

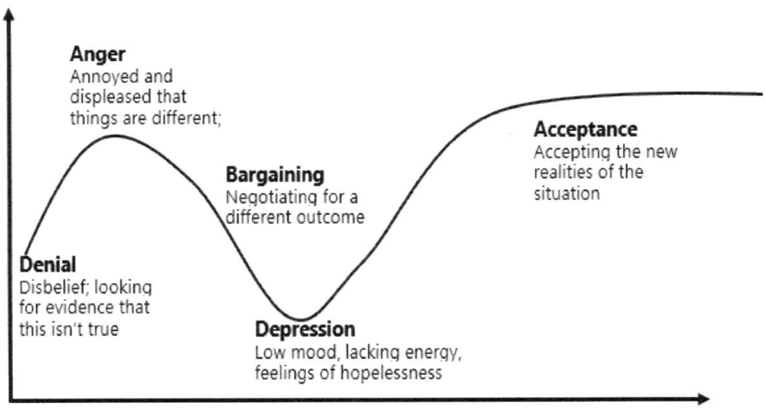

Denial: *Is this really happening? This can't be happening! This happens to other people, not me.* We have all experienced moments of shock and disbelief when a life-changing event presents itself. There's a period of surreal confusion where you are trying to process what you have just learned and then immediately start thinking of how this is a mistake.

Anger: Feelings of frustration set in when we realize this really is happening and things are going to be different. Finding someone, or anyone or anything, to be angry at is very normal in this stage.

Bargaining: *If only...what if?...I will do anything to make this change not happen.* During the bargaining phase, we are still living in the past and will often try to negotiate our way out of feeling the hurt from this loss.

Depression: Low energy, sadness, hopelessness, self-doubt, and fear, are just a few of the adjectives used to describe depression. Comedian Sarah Silverman describes depression as: "It feels like you are really homesick, but you are already home."

Acceptance: When we begin to realize these changes are permanent, we start to accept the new realities of the situation. We may not like it, but we start to accept it. During this stage, we experiment with new things and adjust to our new normal.

I also studied this exact model while studying organizational change in graduate business school. The model is used in business to help employees deal with change that occurs within the organization. Leadership uses the model to identify which stages employees will go through as they grieve over changes affecting them and the work they do. Employees will often be educated on the stages so they are prepared for changes and, hopefully, can move on to the next stage as quickly as possible—getting everyone back to business as usual. Change is always a very volatile time for any organization. It is normal to expect disruptions, frustrations, and some resistance. In most organizations, leaders are taught how to use the change management program, and they decide what needs to be changed based on new regulations, performance measures, new services, etc. Once the project is well underway, a few select, high-performing employees, or in some cases the only employees who would volunteer, are added to the project team to help work out the last of the details, plan the rollout, and share the changes with the rest of the employees to get their buy-in. For the vast majority of employees within the organization, however, change feels like being invited to the party at the very end, just before it's time to clean up the mess.

"Somewhere, someone is changing something...and it's going to affect you," is what one employee told me she took away from a short presentation I gave to a group of 150 employees. I was telling them for the first time that budget cuts were forcing a hiring freeze and there were going to be some changes. If you have never been in this situation of impending change, your heart feels like it is going to bust out of your chest and life flashes by in your head. You don't even really know if it is going to be a good or a bad change for you, but you are already freaked out, so it doesn't even matter at the time whether it's good or bad because you stopped listening as soon as you heard the word "change."

So imagine this.... Imagine the massive amount of change that takes place in our organizations each year. Imagine how many people are experiencing change in their work environments (we won't even mention the struggles these people could be having in their personal worlds) on a regular basis. Imagine the vast majority of employees in a company going through the stages of grieving with every change that takes place in their workplace. So think about this, even the most successful organizations in the world fail in their change efforts 50 to 80 percent of the time. That's a lot of grief and a not-so-impressive track record. So why do we keep changing the same way despite a low outcome? I can't answer this, but I can tell you that I have watched organizations continually repeat their same mistakes over and over and over again when trying to create change, despite the negative effects it has on the employees and their wellbeing. Nothing lets employees know you don't really care about them more than continually making bad changes in their work area and not even including them in it.

Maybe it's not *change* that's so bad; maybe it's *being changed.*

The majority of us are never taught, formally or informally, how to create effective change. We learn about change through life experiences—watching our parents and others, who were most likely never taught effective change management skills either; and by watching TV, movies, cartoons, and even the news. It doesn't matter how old or how young we are, how rich or poor, the color of our skin.... We are going to experience change many times throughout our lives as we grow into who and what we want to become—as we adjust to the unexpected twists, turns, and obstacles thrown at us. Most of us won't get the opportunity to learn how to create successful change at work either; instead, we will be taught how to deal with it.

What if we could start learning how to create successful change habits when we are young so that by the time we are entering the workforce, we are already in the habit of creating effective change? I kept asking myself this question over and over when I saw the massive benefit to understanding how to create effective change in life as the bigger picture to being able to create change at work and most certainly bigger than being dragged through bad change over and over at work. I see an enormous problem for society if the vast majority of people in every organization are in grief-related stages due to bad organizational change. I also see an enormous opportunity for organizations to start being the solution! I believe we can change better together.

It's time to change the change curve; okay, maybe not change it, but at least add another option where knowledge and understanding foster optimism and courage....

When you feel experienced and confident in your ability to be still and make the right next move, feelings of anger, fear, and uncertainty may be replaced with optimism and courage. That's not to say that you won't experience anger, or go back and forth between anger and courage. Courage is embedded in the skills of self-awareness. While bargaining is about staying in the past to look for solutions, planning is about looking forward and planning what comes next. Confidence is experienced when you achieve new challenges and experiment with new activities. The feelings we experience when we feel confident are almost indescribable. It feels so good—the opposite of what depression feels like!

Courage is what happens when we can overcome fear and self-doubt, which give way to depression when we can't or won't make the changes we need to make to get to a new normal. Acceptance of the new norm and integration of new activities into normal day-to-day life help hardwire our practices and turn them into habits. Experimenting with new thoughts, ideas, and behaviors helps us adjust and adapt to our new situation. So think about this: Your kid has just been through a big change, maybe a breakup, a bullying incident, or the loss of a friendship. Would you rather your child go through the change from a place of depression or from a place of courage? Courage numbs the pain we feel with the same dopamine chemicals that opioids numb the pain with. Current research shows increasing levels of depression, addiction, anxiety, and loneliness in our children and decreasing levels of self-confidence, courage, and empathy. Life has many distinct fork in the road of life. What's next depends on what you do at this point. What new behaviors will you integrate into your life?

KNOW BETTER, CHANGE BETTER

Change continues to be one of the most written about and spoken about subjects there is. From the personal self-help section to the business section, there is a plethora of information on creating change. I started studying change in the organizational setting (or so I thought) about a decade ago. This was about the time I got my Lean Six Sigma certification. If you have no idea what Lean Six Sigma is, don't worry; I didn't either. Lean Six Sigma is a tool or method used by organizations to manage their performance and productivity. It is so well respected as a useful tool for generating successful outcomes that 100 percent of the Fortune 500 Companies have some form of it built into their management structures. It is a phenomenal tool for time management, goal setting, managing finances, goal achievement, and a lot of other important things you should know when you want to perform your best at home and at work. It is about aligning your actions to your end goals. It is about effective and efficient use of resources (time, energy, money) to work smarter rather than harder.

When I realized how good Lean Six Sigma is for organizing, improving, and achieivng, I started using it in my personal life. Let me tell you…my actions were so efficient and effective that eight months into my self-proclaimed "Year of Toie," I managed to find time to meet, get engaged, and marry an Englishman, all while I was working full-time, earning my MBA, running my small group home, and single-parenting two boys. My performance and productivity were off the charts, which would have been fantastic if my thoughts had been in the right place too. They weren't, and that's when I discovered the first part of creating successful change. The part that comes before our actions. The part that actually guides our actions. The part that helps us see the right problems so we can also see and achieve the right possibilities. You know—connecting our thoughts with our actions to achieve our best outcomes.

For years, we believed that happiness was the result of our success. But Shawn Achor, Harvard professor and author of the *New York Times* bestseller *The Happiness Advantage*, reveals that his research conducted on students at Harvard indicated it is actually the opposite—happiness leads to success. Achor was the guest on one of the first episodes I watched of *SuperSoul Sunday*. When I heard his story, I felt like purple smoke had just blown out of the top of my head. Achor applied to Harvard on a dare, got in as a student, and stayed there for twelve years studying and researching depression among students. He admits it sounds crazy to think about students at Harvard being depressed when they have so much opportunity in front of them. But, as Achor explained, most Harvard students were accustomed to being at the top of their class. At Harvard, all but one of them lost that status, and 50 percent were below average for the first time in their lives. This is a big change to deal with, and coupled with the intense pressure of school work, it caused depression for many of the students.

Achor conducted hundreds of interviews over several years and discovered an advantage that some of the students had over others—a set of skills that helped them thrive when many others in the same environment were just surviving and even struggling. He calls it the "happiness advantage," and the advantage starts with how you see things. Focusing on positive thoughts or negative thoughts brings positive or negative experiences into your life. It is the Law of Attraction, and it is based on the idea that people and their thoughts are both made from pure energy and like energy attracts more like energy. Replacing self-destructive and self-limiting thoughts with more empowering and adaptive thoughts through creative visualization, practicing gratitude, and other mindful practices can help you get and stay on the positive side of your life where you can see the possibilities. There really is an advantage to being happy; those who see the glass as half-full enjoy that advantage. The good news is, even if you are a glass half-empty kind of thinker, you can develop a more optimistic approach to life and gain the happiness advantage others have by adopting some of the healthy habits your optimistic friends have developed. Being optimistic isn't just about being happy all the time; it's about having the ability to see opportunities where others just see problems. The ability to see the opportunity beyond the problem opens the door to solutions, growth, innovation, and success. It's the starting point for everything that comes next. This important set of skills that Achor identifies is part of the Emotional Intelligence skill sets. In fact, these skills are primarily all self-awareness skills. This is important because the vast majority of organizations (and schools) overlook these skills as part of the foundational skills for creating empathy, collaboration, adaptability, and leadership. The second chapter of this book is dedicated to Emotional Intelligence.

Gallup research studies cite work as the primary source of stress for most Americans, with coworkers, bosses, and unreasonable demands listed as the top three things causing chronic stress and all the health issues associated with it.

Maya Angelou once said, "When you know better, you can do better." It is an exciting time to see the changes organizations are making as we continue to discover what makes people thrive, engage, and perform in life and at work. My hope is that one day organizations will teach all of their employees how to create successful change, not just so they can be included in change projects at work, but because the ability to create positive change in their personal lives is the best investment and gift you can give to yourself and the people you care about. I also hope schools will incorporate these Social and Emotional Learning skills into their learning curriculum for K-12 so our children and grandchildren can learn these skills and create these habits at an early age.

HARDWIRING HABITS

Creating long-lasting successful change is about hardwiring your new habits before your discipline muscle wears out and you revert back to your old habits. I feel sure that I don't have to describe how difficult it can be when you are transitioning from old habits to new habits. We are going to discuss how to overcome this in later chapters, but for now, I want you to think about creating habits of continual growth. When I first started studying change, I was coming at it from an organizational change perspective. When I realized that organizational change and personal development are connected and achieved in the same way, I developed one method that works for achieving any kind of change. There are hundreds of thousands of books on change. They all are based on fundamental knowledge and practices presented in a variety of different ways. If you understand the fundamentals of change, know the 5 Steps to Change (covered below), and practice developing your skills, you can create habits of continual growth that you can master over a lifetime. That means you effectively also master the skills required to create successful change, like emotional intelligence, empathy, self-awarenss, self-confidence, courage, adaptability, process improvement, project management, and of course, change management. Hardwiring continual growth habits helps us to feel confident we can create the right next move even in difficult and distressing situations.

CHANGE EDUCATION

Now that you know how important change is in our lives, let me ask you this: When did you learn about change? Did you take a class or learn about it in school? Did you know there is a change curve? Did you know there are only 5 Steps to Change and they have been the same for hundreds of years? Probably not because most of us are not formally or informally taught how to manage change effectively. So, if change is important (and it is), and habits are created by repeating the same action or process over and over (which they are), what would happen if we could create positive change habits? Change management is like any skill—it gets better the more we practice it. If you were going to speak in front of a large crowd, play an instrument in front of an audience, or play any sport, you would practice. You would practice a lot so when it was your time to perform, you were in the habit of performing. Your speech would practically flow out of your mouth, your fingers would find the right chord at the right time, and you'd hit nothing but net at the big game. However, the practice that led up to the big event would have been anything but perfect, especially in the beginning. You didn't start out running. You started out crawling, then walking, then running. Incorporating programs like mine that focus on Social and Emotional Learning are becoming more and more popular in many K-12 schools across the country. Such programs reduce bullying and absenteeism while increasing academic performance and the overall wellbeing of the students and staff.

THE CHANGING BRAIN

Until the last few decades, scientists believed the only changing our brains did after childhood was starting to decline and lose brain cells. As it turns out, the brain does not stop growing in adulthood; it can grow throughout our entire lifespans. In fact, every time we learn a new fact or skill, we change our brain. It's called neuroplasticity. Our brain is one amazing machine. We don't even fully understand what it is capable of. It holds all of our history and the key to our future at the same time. Our brain's ability to create new neural pathways brings new hope for the treatment of brain injuries and brain diseases. It also causes us to stop and think about the way we learn and work. Psychologists and neuroscientists continue to study the brain, collaborating in research to understand how our brain functions throughout the day in different situations, circumstances, and environments. Bringing a new understanding and appreciation for creating an environment where people (students, employees, teachers, customers) can thrive.

HOW WELL DO WE SCORE AT CHANGE?

If you have already ditched your New Year's or Back to School resolutions, or you can't even remember what they were, you're not alone. Popular studies indicate that only 8 percent of New Year's resolutions are maintained for longer than a year. You might think organizations score a lot higher than individuals in their change success rates. Well, they do, but not by much. According to an article in the *Huffington Post*, even among the most successful organizations, change efforts fail 50 to 80 percent of the time. This is why we need to start thinking about change a little differently—so we can understand how change works, learn the formula, practice the formula anywhere, and create habits of personal development and continual growth. As Albert Einstein said, "The definition of insanity is doing the same thing over and over again, but expecting different results."

EXERCISES

A popular saying, often attributed to Albert Einstein, Henry Ford, or Mark Twain, is worth repeating: "If you always do what you've always done, then you are going to get what you've always got."

Are you ready to look at the world a little differently? Are you ready to get to know yourself a little better? Are you ready to start creating the habits and life you really want? Are you ready to stop working hard and start working smart to make time every day to do the things that help you thrive? Changing is part of living. To ignore change is to bury your head in the sand and hope you grow a sunflower out your back side to provide shelter for you when it rains. Accepting the Change Curve as the best way to manage change for fifty years is only slightly less absurd! (Sorry, Dr. Kübler-Ross; I mean no disrespect. Your work is profoundly relevant even after so many decades, but surely you thought people would continue to develop your model to include new research and theories.) Answer the questions below to start thinking about change and achieving possibilities a little differently. You are worth it!

Answer these questions:

1. When was the last time I did something for the first time? What was it?

____

____

____

2. When was the last time I really impressed with something I did? What was it?

____

____

____

3. If I could do anything I wanted, what kind of work would I do?

____

____

____

4. If I were going to create the perfect day, what would it be?

____

____

____

5. When was the last time I felt confident and courageous? What was I doing?

____

____

____

CHAPTER TWO

THRIVING TO REACH ENDLESS POSSIBILITIES

"My mission in life is not merely to survive, but to thrive; and to do so with some passion, some compassion, some humor, and some style."

— Maya Angelou

CONNECTING OUR TWO BRAINS

My Sunday evening ritual normally includes watching *America's Funniest Home Videos* while I finish up paperwork from the week. I laugh, I cry sometimes from laughing so hard, and I feel cleansed. You know—like all the bad energy has been laughed right out of me. Last week, there was a clip of a small boy who was probably about three years old. He was receiving a small, electric Jeep for his birthday. His parents had parked it in the garage with a big, blue bow covering the entire windshield. The dad was on the far side of the garage filming his son as he walked into the garage to find his surprise. The mom entered the garage with the boy and waited by the door as the boy walked farther into the garage and closer to his new Jeep. The boy walked right past the Jeep and continued to look hard for his surprise. In fact, at one point, he was looking so hard, his father said, "Is he putting us on?" To which the mother replied, "I know. I wonder how long we should let this go on!" The parents even gave hints to the boy, "You don't see something here in the garage with a big blue bow?" For whatever reason, that sweet little boy could not see the Jeep through the forest, even though it was sitting right there in the middle of his garage with a big, blue bow on it. He was ecstatic once he saw his surprise, and he was very thankful to his parents, who practically wet their pants from laughing before the end.

The Jeep was so obvious to the parents and everyone watching the video, but the boy couldn't see it until he was ready to see it. It had been there all along. I bet the scientists who first discovered what we now call Emotional Intelligence (EQ) probably felt a lot like the parents in this video when they first started seeing EQ in their research. There were no words to describe what they were seeing because no one was looking for another kind of intelligence or had even thought about one existing. Scientists had been studying IQ relentlessly and thinking it was the only kind of intelligence. So, after a hundred-plus years of studying diseases and conditions of the brain that cause suffering, scientists started studying the opposite: What role does our brain play in helping us thrive?

Daniel Goleman popularized the term Emotional Intelligence in the 1990s with his book *Emotional Intelligence: Why It Can Matter More Than IQ*. It quickly became a number one *New York Times* bestseller and is considered the first self-help book based on science. When you read it, you will probably feel like the little boy who couldn't see his new Jeep. I did.

Even though we didn't know what EQ was or have a name for it until the 1990s, we have long recognized the importance of the individual skills involved. It's like having all of the parts to build a toaster, but not knowing what a toaster is. When all of the parts are assembled, they create a toaster to make toast. Individually, the parts...well, they're just parts.

Wow, talk about a zero to hero story. Listen to this.... Two scientists published a research paper which, like most research papers, was read by very few people. Then Daniel Goleman wrote a book and popularized the term EQ in hopes he would see the day when people were talking about EQ in normal conversation.

Fast forward to today.... *EQ is now considered the single most important determinant for life success. Let me repeat that. Emotional Intelligence is the most important skill for you to develop to achieve success in all areas of your life.*

From the schoolroom to the boardroom and everywhere in between, EQ helps us understand our thoughts and emotions so we can manage our actions and behavior to achieve what we want to achieve. It helps us to create and maintain loving relationships; become authentic leaders of ourselves, our families, our communities, and our schools; and even be leaders of successful organizations, if we are into that sort of thing.

While we are born with a certain level of EQ, we can continue to develop and increase it throughout our lifetimes. EQ empowers our ability to overcome negative emotions like fear, anxiety, and anger and maximize the positive emotions that motivate and inspire us to take smart risks to grow into the people we are meant to be. Remember the "Happiness Advantage"? The self-awareness skills that Achor talks about in his book are the foundational skills for EQ.

Dr. Travis Bradberry, psychologist and co-writer of the *New York Times* best-selling book, *Emotional Intelligence 2.0*, says this about EQ in the business environment: "Emotional intelligence and earnings are so direct that for every point increase in EQ, annual salary increases by $1,300." Bradberry says the link between performance, pay, and emotional intelligence is directly linked across all industries, at all levels of organizations, in every region of the world.

Goleman says EQ, though relatively new in the world of science, is responsible for up to 80 percent of success, while IQ is responsible for about 4 to 10 percent.

THE FOUR DOMAINS OF EMOTIONAL INTELLIGENCE

Emotional Intelligence can be broken down into four separate domains: Self-Awareness, Self-Management, Social Awareness, and Relationship Management. I'll devote an entire part to each of these domains in Parts 2-5, but for now, let's look at a few key details. Each of the four domains list the skills important to mastering that domain before moving on to the next domain. You don't have to be a master at all of the skills listed to move on. In fact, as you learn and experience new things, you might find yourself at the bottom of the learning curve if you are entering a new career, learning a new hobby, or doing anything where you are beginning to learn.

The left side of the diagram below involves self-competence skills: Self-Awareness and Self-Management. These influence how we see and understand ourselves and lead our actions. The right side of the diagram involves social competence: Social Awareness and Relationship Management. These influence how we see and understand others and how we manage relationships. Self-Awareness is in the top, left corner in the *king spot.* If you are familiar with the popular elementary school recess game four square, you know the person occupying the *king spot* initiates every action in the game. Similarly, our thoughts initiate all of the actions that follow, so it's important to have self-awareness—to be aware of our thoughts and emotions. Thoughts are *king* and the buck starts here, in the top, left corner.

Arrows lead down to Self-Management and across to Social Awareness. Relationship Management is in the bottom, right corner. Our ability to manage meaningful relationships in our personal and professional lives is determined by our level of skill in all four domains. The buck stops here. We are all born with a unique mix of skill levels in all of the domains. We all have superhero skills in some areas and lame skills in others. The good news is we can improve our skills in any area by practicing those skills.

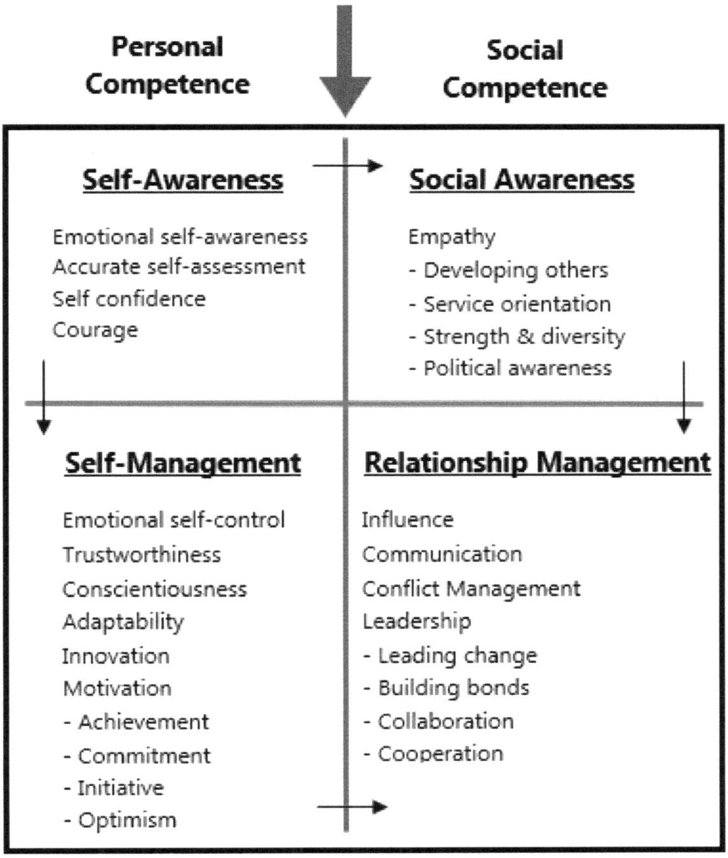

Here's a brief description of each of the four domains. We will discuss each of them in much more detail in the following chapters.

Self-Awareness: Knowing who you are and what you value. Self-confidence, courage, and accurate self assessment are some of the skills of self-awareness. Our thoughts and experiences shape our morals and values and how we see ourselves and our world. Self-Awareness is the foundation for all of the other EQ skills. Understanding our own feelings helps us to understand others' feelings.

Self-Management: Managing ourselves and our actions to achieve what we want to achieve. Skills like motivation, adaptability, trustworthiness, and optimism are important for achieving goals and dreams, and they are often part of the core values of schools and organizations.

Social Awareness: Understanding and sensing others' feelings, needs, and concerns. It is the capacity for understanding what others are saying and feeling and why they feel and act as they do. Empathy is the primary skill of social awareness.

Relationship Management: Working well with others and maintaining meaningful relationships (personal and professional). Leadership is happening everywhere, not just at work. The skills to inspire others and manage conflict to create the best outcomes can be used with family, friends, neighbors, teammates, classmates, coworkers, spouses, and children.

ARE WE BECOMING LESS CIVILIZED?

Whether it's on the news, social media, or in person, you don't have to go very far to witness people being swept away by emotion and behaving in ways they will most likely regret when they are thinking more clearly. We see reports of people punching people over parking spaces, parents fighting on the sidelines at their children's sporting events, police officers using unexplained and excessive force, flight attendants going at it with passengers, fast food workers and customers duking it out, and kids shooting their classmates—just to name a few. So what's going on? And more importantly, what can we do about it? Here's my theory...

We have two brains: our thinking brain and our feeling brain.

Our feeling brain, also known as our primitive or emotional brain, was around long before our thinking brain. It acts as an information regulator. It does not think or learn, but, instead, keeps our bodies functioning like they should. All of our memories and emotions are stored in the primitive brain.

The amygdala region of the primitive brain is in the optimal spot for seeing and hearing all incoming information before it reaches any other areas of the brain. This little almond-shaped region is designed to respond lightning-quick in an emergency. If the information is not urgent, the amygdala assesses it and passes it on to the other parts of the brain where we can think about how we want to react. This allows us to think about how we feel before we react.

The amygdala takes care of actions that are too important to rely on thinking, like jumping out of the way of a moving car, freezing when you hear a snake or burglar, pulling your hand away from a hot stove, and jumping back when someone jumps out to scare you. It's called fight, flight, or freeze. In these emergent situations, there is no time to think about removing your hand from the hot stove or pondering what kind of snake you heard. There is no time to think. The amygdala processes information very quickly so we can respond very quickly.

Here lies the problem.... The amygdala processes information super-fast, but it provides a sloppy, incomplete assessment of the situation—the amygdala is not looking for accuracy. If we react before our thinking brain can get involved with the situation, we are letting the primitive part of the brain dictate our actions and behaviors. Think of the amygdala as your own personal bodyguard...only instead of Kevin Costner, you get a Neanderthal with lightning-quick reflexes and no ability to think. Your Neanderthal bodyguard sits poised and ready to pounce, freeze, or flee at the slightest hint of a threat (real or perceived). The problem is that he doesn't really understand the common modern-day threats we experience on a regular basis. Modern threats are less about getting eaten by a saber-tooth tiger and more about making enough money to pay your mortgage, feed your kids, and pay for your healthcare, or navigating bullies in school or the workplace.

Emotional Intelligence skills help us create communication between our two brains so our thoughts, actions, and behaviors are aligned with who we are and what we want to achieve. When we respond quickly without thinking, our Pleistocene bodyguard is in charge without any involvement from our thinking brain. This would definitely make us appear to be less civilized! Mel Robbins, author, life coach, and CNN reporter, once said, "Your life is defined by the gap between what happens to you and your reaction to it." Your EQ is what creates that gap. The more EQ you have, the less often your uncivilized bodyguard will take over your body and embarrass you or change the course of your life with actions and words you can't take back later when you take a minute to think about how you really want to respond to the situation.

THRIVE ON

Thrive: to grow vigorously, flourish, or to progress toward or realize a goal despite or because of circumstances (Merriam Webster). Some of the most dreaded and miserable circumstances can bring about the most tremendous growth and transformation. In my twenty years of working as a registered nurse (RN), I have had the opportunity to work in many different disciplines. My favorite areas were hospice and oncology. Many might think of these as pretty sad places to work, but I loved them. Although my patients were dying, they were alive and grateful to be alive—more alive and more grateful than most of the people walking around this planet without any thought as to what their purposes are.

I believe every living thing was created for a purpose. What's your purpose? You had a *one-in-four-trillion* chance of being born, and you did it. Congratulations! Now what are you meant to be doing to fulfill your purpose?

In the many conversations I have had with people who have come close to death and lived to tell about it—those who were just starting to dance with the angels, those who could see the white lights, and those who described feeling fire at their feet—they all wanted their loved ones by their side. They all fully appreciated life and the time, long or short, they had left. Most of them had at least a few more things they wanted to do—some had many. Some of them wanted to talk about their families, some about their accomplishments and the obstacles they had overcome. Not one of them said they would have worked more or cared what they were wearing or what kind of car they drove.

INNOVATIVE FUNDAMENTALS: SEVEN AREAS OF LIFE

We all have heard by now that we need balance, but what exactly are we supposed to be balancing? What do we need to balance to be at our best? Just like an organization has designated which departments are essential for it to function and thrive, such as HR, finance, management, and customer service, we also have areas of our lives that are essential for our success in life. These areas function in the same way as departments within an organization. If you think about where you work, the departments all have individual functions, responsibilities, and goals, and they all work together and rely on each other to achieve their larger organizational purpose. The key areas of life work together in much the same way to help us achieve our goals and overall purpose.

The seven areas are:

1. Work
2. Finances
3. Family
4. Physical Health
5. Education
6. Social Network
7. Emotional Health

Let's now look at each one in more detail.

1. Work (Job/Career/Calling): Do you get excited when it is time to go to work? Okay, maybe not excited, but do you look forward to Monday morning, or do you start dreading it on Sunday afternoon? As previously mentioned, people continually list work as the primary source of stress in their lives, with coworkers, bosses, and unreasonable demands being the primary causes of that stress. The other day, a man I met in the elevator was telling me a story about an unreasonable demand he encounters every day at work. He works for a large telephone company, and in the morning when he gets to work, he and all of the other workers have to do a quick, detailed inspection of their trucks and fill out a form verifying they inspected them. He explained that it takes about fifteen minutes to do the inspection, fill out the form, and hand in the form. "The problem," he said as he chuckled, "is we can only be in the truck yard for ten minutes in the mornings." He went on to talk about the separation between leadership and the field crew. Management had been consolidated in another town, and since the consolidation, most of the leaders have come from the business world, not from the field, so when they change the way things work in the field, they don't always make sense or solve the problem the change was meant to solve. With no chance of advancement and ridiculous demands, the man said he was just working for the paycheck at this point.

If the best thing about the work you do is the paycheck, then you probably have a job rather than a calling. A job is a paid position of regular employment. It pays the bills, but it doesn't get you excited and rarely gets 100 percent of your best effort. There's a big difference between having a job and having a job you enjoy and are good at. It's a mindset of renting rather than owning…you know, partially committed. You may work with people like this. In fact, research shows you definitely work with people like this, which is probably why coworkers are at the top of the list of stressors.

A career is an occupation undertaken for a significant period of a person's life with opportunities for progress. A career usually requires education or advanced learning of some kind, but that is not always the case. A career isn't about a title; it's about a mindset. How do you feel about the work you do? What does it mean to you?

Helia is a housekeeper on the fourth floor of one of the hospitals where I worked. She has been a housekeeper there for twenty years—it is her calling. She loves it. The hospital has tuition assistance and work-school programs it has offered to Helia and other employees interested in furthering their education, but Helia has never been interested in signing up for nursing, physical therapy, or radiology. When I asked her why she decided to stay in housekeeping, she told me she loves what she does and doesn't want the hassle and stress the other departments have. She enjoys visiting with the patients and feels like she makes a difference in helping them get better by keeping their rooms clean and fresh. She isn't on the list of direct care staff, but she is one of the hospital's most valuable assets. She is important to the staff and the patients. In fact, whenever patients bring in cupcakes, muffins, donuts, or anything else we shouldn't eat but love to, the card always includes Helia's name among those thanked as part of the healing team. Housekeeping is Helia's career—her calling.

A calling is a strong urge toward a particular way of life—a career, a vocation. It is not about the pay or the title—it's about the way you feel about what you are doing and your commitment to it. A calling comes from your actions being aligned with your purpose, and joy is what you feel as you get to experience the fruits of your labor. A calling is about knowing what you value and creating an environment in which it can thrive.

Many of us get stuck in the job phase because we enjoy having roofs over our heads and we need to eat. Living paycheck to paycheck can suck the dreams right out of your head if you are not careful. If you are in a job now but want more meaningful work, practice your mindfulness. Can you be the catalyst to creating the change you want to see? If the environment you are working in hasn't yet figured out how to create a culture of respect, confidence, and compassion where everyone can thrive and work together, then you could be that catalyst. If your work environment is better at tearing people down than building them up, start thinking about what you really want to do. What deserves my valuable time and efforts? How does my work fit into my balanced life? Am I making a difference? Can I afford to do what I really want to do?

The work we do and how we do it says a lot about who we are. The work we choose dictates many aspects of our lives, including our schedule, the neighbourhood we live in, and even the hobbies and vacations we can or cannot afford. We spend significant time at work, and the people and environment there influence our mood and overall wellbeing. When we are enjoying our work to the extent that our actions seem effortless and we perform at our top ability, we are in a state of flow. Athletes and artists describe this state as "being in the zone." The workplace is the number one place for experiencing flow.

2. Finances: Managing our financial life is the second highest cause of stress in the United States. Job uncertainties, increased debt, reduced retirement, and escalating medical expenses have many people worrying about having enough money to live on. In fact, most Americans are living in debt. How we spend our money and manage our finances is heavily influenced by our habits—habits we learned from watching others manage their finances. Our parents are the biggest influence on how we spend, save, and make money. When our income meets or exceed our needs, we feel secure.

People often think being rich means having a big house and a fancy car. If you are into big houses and fancy cars, and you can afford them, and they bring you joy, then you are rich. Equally, if your three-bedroom, modest, 1971 ranch-style house brings you joy, and you can afford it, and you feel secure about your finances, you are rich too. Rich is not a number. It is how you feel about your financial situation.

About twenty years ago, I needed a sign painted to go on the front of a building. It was the old days before the internet, so I was looking in the telephone book to find a sign painter. I found a man named John who showed up to the building in an old, beat-up Volkswagen van. He had long, dark-blond hair and wore old jeans and an old shirt with paint of all colors on them. When he opened the doors to his van, I noticed he had an off-road motorcycle in the back wedged between paint cans, paint buckets, and a large shelf of brushes of all sizes. When I asked John about the bike, he said he takes a two-hour lunch every day and finds a place to ride his bike for a little while. He had been doing it for years, ever since he left his corporate finance job. He said he has never been happier. John admitted it was not easy in the beginning without his corporate salary. He had to adjust his lifestyle and redefine what was important to him. But with his kids grown and out of the house, he found he didn't require as much money to be happy, and he prefers to make less and ride his bike every day while creating artful signs. John said that before he changed his focus, his finances were managing him. He felt like he had to keep working to feed the beast. He hadn't enjoyed working in finance for several years, but he had stayed because he had kids in college and bills to pay, retirement to save for, and so on. He took medication for high blood pressure, high cholesterol, and pre-diabetes. One day at work, he looked around and said to himself, "I believe my work here is done." He described it as an out-of-body experience, like watching someone else giving his notice to his boss. John said the feeling of *next* had been building up inside him, and it was time for what came *next*. Within a few months of leaving his job, he was able to get off most of his medications. John liked to joke that he didn't really learn to manage his finances until he retired from his finance job.

3. Family: Our first and deepest connections are with our family members. They know us best and we know them best. While it is comforting to have someone who knows you and cares about you when you are not feeling well, it is not fun to fight with a family member who knows all of your weaknesses and insecurities. The connections that develop from eating meals together, laughing and crying together, and sharing our feelings are deep connections, capable of stirring up extreme emotions—both positive and negative. Healthy relationships with parents, siblings, spouses, and children can bring joy and happiness. Sometimes, jealousy, fear, anger, sadness, guilt, or resentment can sour relationships quicker than Jerry Springer's bodyguards can get across the stage. The loss of a significant relationship, whether from divorce, death, or an argument, is the fourth leading cause of stress in the United States.

4. Physical Health: The *Huffington Post* reports, "Only 8 percent of people actually keep their New Year's resolutions." Improving our physical health is at the top of the list when it comes to making our New Year's resolutions. We promise to eat better, exercise more, worry less, quit smoking, start eating kale, and maybe even meditate. Thoughts and practices related to physical health have changed at a staggering pace over the years. It has become hard to keep track of what we should or should not be eating, which app is better, and which vitamins we should be taking for this or that; then once we get that all figured out, we have to figure out how to make time in our busy schedules to give our bodies the attention they need to be healthy and support us as we reach for our dreams. The United States falls behind most other developed countries in terms of physical health, largely due to lifestyle choices, eating habits, and chronic stress. The cost of stress on our bodies is significant, so learning to manage stress effectively can dramatically improve our physical health. Physical health is the third leading cause of stress in the United States.

5. Education: Education includes spending time to learn and experience new things. It can be formal or informal. A few years ago, I finally took the oil painting class I had been wanting to take. It was the first non-school or work-related education I had done for myself in years... and it was amazing to take it with my mom and grandma. I wish I had done it years earlier. What we choose to spend our time learning says a lot about who we are and what is important to us. Bill Gates, Elon Musk, Mark Cuban, Mark Zuckerberg, and Oprah Winfrey all read several books each month, but not just any kinds of books. They aren't keeping up with the Kardashians or the real housewives of wherever. They are highly selective about what they read and generally read educational, rather than entertaining, books. They are at the top of their games, and they continue to be curious and have the desire to continue growing. We have so many things we can choose to spend our time on. Knowing what is important to us can help us create moments, days, years, and decades of learning and experiences that will inspire us, educate us, and challenge us to think in new and different ways. When we are passionate and enjoy what we are learning about, we can experience a state of flow.

6. Social Network: Dan Buettner, explorer, journalist, and *New York Times* bestselling author of *Blue Zones*, has been working with National Geographic and others to study the areas around the world with the highest populations of centenarians (people who have lived 100 years or more). Along with a healthy plant-based diet, he found that people who have a purpose and can articulate it live about seven years longer than those who don't have a clear purpose. People who belong to a faith-based community and attend a service each week live four to fourteen years longer than those who don't. Many centenarians believe their wine each night has kept them feeling spry and active. Buettner discovered that none of the centenarians exercise like we think of exercising, but instead, they lead more active lives all around. They burn more calories during usual activities and do not sit at a desk all day.

Buettner found that social relationships were a common thread among all of the centenarians. Studies show that in the 1950s, people had on average three good friends they could have meaningful conversations with, trust, and confide in, and that they really liked. Today's statistics show most Americans only have 1.5 good friends. Another study found that in 1950, the average onset age of depression was 29.5 years, but now it's 14.5. In doing research for his book *The Happiness Advantage*, Achor found that our social network is as important to our wellbeing as the condition of our heart and lungs. Whom you spend your time with directly affects the quality of your life. If your friends have healthy habits, you are more likely to have healthy habits.

Bill George, Harvard business professor, former CEO of Medtronic, and author of the *New York Times* bestseller *True North*, is well known as a pioneer in authentic leadership. In a presentation to Stanford graduates, he revealed that he is part of a men's group that meets once a week on Wednesday mornings from 7:15 to 8:30. About a dozen men are in the group, and usually seven or eight show up each time to gather and talk. They share stories and advise and support each other when needed. They are to George what a board of directors is intended to be for an organization. They are people who care about each other's success and bring valuable experiences to each other. They all have unique strengths and viewpoints that provide information to be shared freely and without judgment.

Our closest friends know our habits and can see our blind spots, even when we are unaware of them. If we think and plan according to what we know, we are underestimating the power of our habits. Close friends know how to let us know kindly that we have lipstick on our teeth or shaving cream on our ear, that our skirt is tucked into our underwear, our fly is open, or we keep dating Mr./Ms. Wrong or even cousin Way Wrong. Friends see all of that, but until you learn to see that, too, you will continue to make the same mistakes over and over.

By the way, George's group has been meeting since the 1970s. His wife also has a group of friends she has met with for years. Loneliness, sadness, and depression can occur in the absence of meaningful relationships, no matter how many Facebook friends you may have! We thrive when we have at least one good friend we can call in the middle of the night if we need them.

Having supportive, loving relationships is vital to our wellbeing. We all have a sense of longing to feel like we belong and are valued. Connecting with others is a basic human instinct, and who we spend our time with greatly affects the quality of our lives and the choices we make. In the Bible, King Solomon said, "He that walketh with wise men shall be wise: but a companion of fools shall be destroyed" (Proverbs 13:20). We could put that in modern language as "Show me your friends and I will show you your future." Spending time with good friends causes our bodies to release a chemical called serotonin into our blood supply. Serotonin contributes to our feelings of wellbeing and happiness.

7. Emotional Health: The health of our emotions is vital to our success in all areas of life. Our emotions influence everything we think, do, and say. They move us into action, and if we don't manage them, they will control us. Henry Ford once said, "Whether you think you can or you think you can't, you're right." Staying aware of our emotions allows us to keep negative emotions like fear, anger, jealousy, and sadness from hijacking our goals, dreams, and happiness. The origin of such modern-day words as motive, motif, motion, motivation, emotion, and motor is the Latin word *movere*, which means to move. Our emotions are what move us. They move us where we want to go, they move us where we don't really want to go, and sometimes they move us in directions we are not even aware of. However, we can manage our emotions so they don't control us.

INNOVATIVE FUNDAMENTALS SEVEN AREAS MAN (SAM)

SAM stands for the seven areas man. He represents the seven areas of life in a visual picture that is easy to learn and remember. Visual pictures help us understand things better and allow our brains to process information and store it. Think about this: If I mention that I saw a purple horse with a long red tail, does your mind create a picture of a purple horse with a red tail? It probably did because our minds are wired that way. In studying change for over a decade, I found the biggest advantage that organizational change methods have over the vast majority of personal change methods is the robust tools and techniques they use to improve and measure actions. They use organizational charts, dashboard reports, goal reports, progress reports, and monitor reports to track their progress. SAM might appear to be a simple outline drawing of a person, but he actually serves the same purpose as all of the reports listed above. One of my main purposes for creating the Innovative Fundamentals approach is to offer a program that is powerful and based in science while being easy enough for children to start learning at an early age. Think about this—your kindergartener can draw SAM and begin to understand that life is made up of many different things like, friends, family, education, etc….

SAM makes it easy to learn and remember the seven areas of life that are important for achieving true success and happiness. There is nothing scientific about where the words are placed on SAM's body, but the order of the words does follow a nifty little pnuemonic I created to help remember the seven areas (you'll find it below). Sam is an important tool throughout this book and is used in all five steps of the Innovative Fundamentals approach to creating successful change.

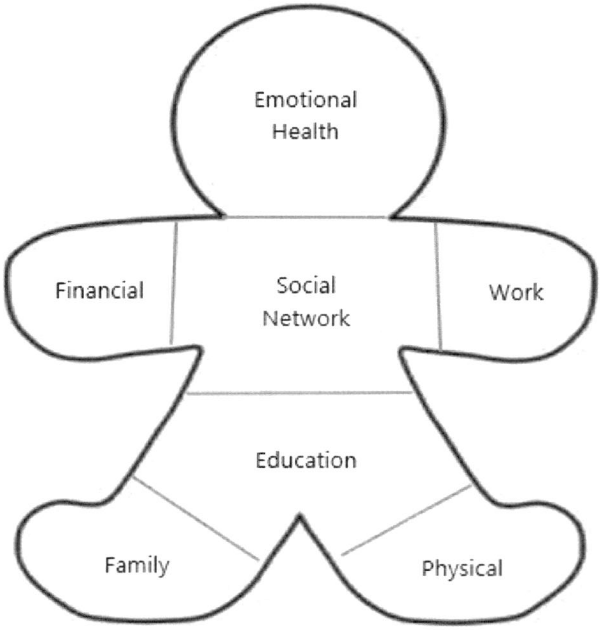

PNEUMONIC FOR SEVEN AREAS MAN (SAM):

Winning (Work)
Feels (Finances)
Fabulous (Family)
Particularly (Physical)
Everyone (Education)
Smiling (Social Network)
Excitedly (Emotions)

Achieving success, even just a little success, feels awesome! The excitement runs through your body and you probably pump your arms in the air, or maybe drop to your knees. You may cry, or maybe you yell... and you most likely smile bigger and longer than usual. Then you share your success with others...and they smile and cheer for you and your win. Winning Feels Fabulous, Particularly Everyone Smiling Excitedly!

EXERCISES

Take some time to get to know yourself a little bit better; you are worth it! Answer the following questions:

Who are the five people I spend the most time with?

____

____

Who has had the most positive influence on my life so far?

____

____

How do I enjoy spending my free time?

____

____

When do I feel I am at my best?

____

____

What new things do I want to learn about?

____

____

Do I feel like I am thriving right now? (Circle answer)

Heck, yeah   I think so   Not yet

Winning Dance: Imagine yourself in your winning situation—even if you have no idea what you are winning at right now. Feel your winning moment like you have achieved a success (any success). Imagine what that moment will feel like. Feel the energy running through your body, pump your arms in the air, yell out loud, drop to your knees, cry tears of joy, jump in the air, and smile like you have never smiled before. Then imagine how good it will feel when others are smiling excitedly with you and for you. These thoughts keep us motivated during the tough times. Your purpose will become clearer and clearer as little successes lead to big successes. Dopamine levels will increase as you continue to envision your success, and your motivation will soar. Practice your winning dance daily and feel how good it feels.

CHAPTER THREE

CONNECTING...WITH YOURSELF AND OTHERS

"Creativity is just connecting things. When you ask creative people how they did something, they feel a little guilty because they didn't really do it, they just saw something. It seemed obvious to them after a while. That's because they were able to connect experiences they've had and synthesize new things."

— Steve Jobs

CONNECTEDNESS

Connectedness is the state or extent of being joined, linked, or connected. Our desire to connect to ourselves, with others, and to our environment are basic human needs. We deeply desire to be connected to things that are bigger than ourselves. We are also very connected to good ole Mother Earth—connected through our reliance on her for everything she provides for us to live and breathe. We are connected by energy. You have probably heard the term "six degrees of separation." It has been around since the late 1920s, and comes from the idea that all living things and everything else in the world are six or fewer steps away from each other. A version of the idea, Six Degrees of Kevin Bacon, was popularized by four college students watching *Footloose* during a heavy snowstorm. It's hard to say whether it was boredom, curiosity, or pure genius, but when Kevin Bacon said he had worked with everybody in Hollywood or someone who had worked with them, these college students turned it into a party game. People would shout out an actor's name and these four friends would figure out how the actor was connected to Kevin Bacon. The number of connections would be described as the person's "Bacon number." This game caught on and has been talked about in multiple movies, ad campaigns, commercials, TV shows, and is even used to describe the most highly connected nodes of the internet, which are referred to as "The 'Kevin Bacons' of the Web."

Connections of all kinds shape and influence the way we live, the way we eat, the way we love, and a lot of times, the jobs we get. Connections are important in all areas. When we feel like we are connected to something bigger than ourselves, we get a sense of belonging and are happier.

Michael Pollan is a journalist, author of four *New York Times* bestsellers, holder of more awards than I can even begin to mention here, and a professor of journalism at UC Berkeley Graduate School of Journalism. For the past twenty-five years, Pollan has been writing about the connections between nature and culture: on our plates, in our farms and gardens, and in the environment we live in. He gives wise and simple advice for eating healthily—like don't eat anything your great-grandma wouldn't recognize as food, and don't get fuel for your body at the same place you get fuel for your car. He practices what he calls mindful eating and celebrates the connection of humans to the earth through the creation of our food. Pollan's writings have helped millions of people worldwide stop and rethink their relationship with food and the choices they make about what goes into their bodies.

Pollan's mindful mindset toward food is the same kind of mindful mindset that brings a deeper understanding and appreciation for the connections that create the bigger picture. It is a mindset that he carries over into all aspects of his life, in the same way we all carry over habits from one area of our lives to the others. I make this point now because given the choice to learn multiple programs that each work on one thing or one program that works on multiple things, most of us would choose to learn one thing. We're not being lazy; our brains are just wired that way. They are designed to conserve energy. Our mind daydreams and zones out throughout our day when it needs a rest. One of the ways our brain conserves energy is by using connections between its hundreds of billions of neurons. These are called neural pathways. They are the super-highways, boulevards, and country roads that connect what we are seeing with what we already know so we can function and survive in our world. Our neural pathways are like muscles, and they get larger and stronger with use. As they get used more often, they become the super-highways of information we call habits.

SEEING NEW CONNECTIONS

Do you remember the last thing you learned that really surprised you? Not like in an, "Oh, my gosh, you scared the *scrap* out of me," or the surprise of friends and family jumping out from behind the couch and curtains to surprise you for your birthday. I'm talking the kind of surprise when, all of the sudden, you see something new you have never seen before, although you have been looking at it for a long time. An "aha moment" when you see something in a deeper way, with more understanding and appreciation of a bigger picture. I had a moment like this working in change management for a large healthcare organization.

I was leading projects across several areas aimed at improving departmental metrics in performance and productivity. As I was looking over their individual departmental goals and initiatives, I saw some connections I had not seen before: All of the departments that dealt with people had empathy-related training with scripting to help staff appear empathetic and, hopefully, learn how to actually be empathetic along the way.

In the service care areas there were framed, decorative signs listing the things patients want from the care staff, like to be heard, included, and understood. In the leadership office areas, there were nicer framed, decorative signs listing the things employees want from their leaders, like to be heard, included, and understood. It's really no surprise that employees and patients want the same thing. In fact, you can find similar lists highlighting what teachers, students, parents, children, spouses, and especially, grandparents want. We all want to be heard, included, and understood. It is a basic human need and desire.

There were also graphs, charts, and diagrams of all shapes, sizes, and colors displaying performance measures. Usually in a green, yellow, and red color scheme to represent good, poor, and bad.

In the operations area, the focus was less on people and more on processes and financial measures. When departments weren't meeting their financial goals, operations was the first to know about it, and generally, a change of some kind would follow. They used process improvement and project management programs like Lean Six Sigma to find the errors and waste, manage resources, measure progress, and set goals aimed at achieving performance and productivity goals.

The quality department focused on all things quality, including all of the performance, quality, and safety indicators. If a department wasn't meeting its quality performance goals, the quality department was the first to know about it, and some kind of education or change would quickly follow.

The frontline or service areas where all these processes were being performed, measured, monitored, and improved were also the same areas where the employees were getting the least amount of education on process improvement and change management. The emotional intelligence HR was trying to teach the employees was actually the first set of skills needed to create successful change. These skills would have been useful for the quality department and operations department to make changes in all the areas they have probably never worked in before. However, if we understand that emotional intelligence skills are the very skills we need to create successful change, then we can understand that by learning how to create successful change, we are developing both our emotional intelligence skills and change management skills at the same time. That means employees could learn to create successful change in their work areas and be included in the changes that affect their work and develop their emotional intelligence skills like empathy, self-confidence, collaboration, and leadership at the same time. More important than the changes we can make at work when understanding how to create successful change are the changes we can create in our personal lives using the same five-step approach. And even more importantly, our children will watch and learn from us as they develop the habits that will guide them the rest of their lives.

CONNECTING WITH YOURSELF

How well do you really know yourself? When you strip away who your parents want you to be, who your grandparents hope you will be, who your neighbors think you are, who your boss expects you to be, and who you are on social media, who are you and why are you here spinning around on this big ball we call Earth?

Over the past few years, I have had several opportunities to discover just how well I didn't know myself. I reluctantly decided I would try out online dating. I wasn't really sure how I was going to like it, but I was living in a new country and didn't really know anyone, so I thought, *What the heck? It works for a lot of people. Maybe I will at least meet some interesting people to hang out with.* I opened a bottle of wine and began the marathon of filling out the lengthy questionnaire about who I am, what I like to do, and who I would like to spend time with.

What do I like to do? Hmm…what *do* I like to do? I listed several things, but struggled to list any hobbies I actually did on a regular basis, or even within the last year. I laughed out loud at myself as I sat there wondering how in the the world I couldn't even think of any current hobbies I was doing. I wasn't sure if I should cry for the time I wasted not being self-aware or jump with joy that at least I realized it then. So, I did both! I had a quick cry, then got busy finding new hobbies like oil painting, hiking, and writing.

CONNECTING WITH OTHERS

Shawn Achor, author of *The Happiness Advantage*, lists having a strong social network as one of the most significant determinants for a long, healthy life—as important to our health as having a healthy heart and lungs. Just hanging out with our friends makes us feel better. We have all experienced how good we feel after spending time talking and laughing with good friends. It refuels us and erases the day's stresses. The science behind this: Serotonin, a chemical similar to dopamine, is released in our brain when we are enjoying the company of friends and family. Serotonin creates feelings of happiness and a sense of belonging—it feels like a great big hug.

Positive social interactions are healthy, natural, and beneficial in the pursuit of happiness. Our ability to create and sustain meaningful relationships depends on our skills in all four of the emotional intelligence domains.

CONNECTING WITH THE WORK WE DO

The majority of us spend most of our time at home, but work usually comes in second—often a very close second. Throughout our lifetimes, we spend an astronomical number of hours in our workplace with our coworkers. The work we do says a lot about who we are and forms a large part of our identity. Many of our friendships are created through our work environment. Our work often determines where we live and shop as well as the hobbies we can afford. Our work determines what education we seek out or get access to. Yet while our work is such a meaningful part of our lives, it continues to be one of the primary causes of stress.

Employees connect with organizations that share their values. This alignment of values helps form the organization's culture and atmosphere. When our work environment feels safe, we can engage with the work we do. If we are at a perfect level of challenge and ability, the work we do is almost effortless and our efficiency is high. We are *in flow*, performing at our peak performance level. Henry Ford never imagined that a successful organization would have bean bag chairs, pool tables, free food, and nap cubicles for employees, but Google, Zappos, and many other widely successful organizations are realizing that thriving people make thriving employees, who are valuable and priceless assets.

While the bean bag chairs and free food are big perks, the culture of inclusion is one of the biggest happiness factors at any organization. We like being included, and not even the most comfortable bean bag chair or the much-needed nap cubicle can replace the feelings we get from being included. It helps us to feel like the work we do is important and that we have value within the organization—like we belong to something bigger than ourselves.

LEARNING THROUGH OUR EXPERIENCES

Do you remember the first *Karate Kid* movie back in 1984? Daniel, the main character, really wanted to learn karate to protect himself from bullies. He couldn't understand why Mr. Miyagi, the little, older, unassuming repairman/martial arts badass, was having him do household chores instead. In fact, Daniel was very offended and upset with Mr. Miyagi until he realized he had been learning and practicing skills he already had; he just needed to learn when to use them. Daniel's relentless repetitions of familiar exercises like waxing the car helped him learn through experiences he already understood and could relate to. Or put more simply, Daniel trained and strengthened his muscles to the point that he could almost automatically execute the moves Miyagi called out from the sidelines at the karate match. This was very helpful for Daniel since he was overwhelmed and barely able to think straight during his first tournament experience. He hadn't become fully confident in his skills yet, and of course, his opponents were very experienced. Miyagi mixed life lessons with Banzai tree trimming, car waxing, dating advice, coat hanging, and winning karate moves. While we understood what Miyagi had done, we left the theater without even knowing we had just been taught about experiential learning and how to apply it. We had just watched Mr. Miyagi teach Daniel karate through experiential rather than traditional methods.

If you didn't see *Karate Kid*, maybe you saw *The Blind Side*, with Sandra Bullock. It is based on the life of professional football player Michael Oher. When Michael started playing high school football, he didn't understand what the coach wanted him to do; he didn't speak football—Michael was a homeless kid, who'd been in and out of the school system. Then Sandra Bullock walks out onto the field, wearing those killer white Capri pants and looking fantastic, and in less than two minutes, she helps Michael understand what the coach had been trying to say for the last week. You see, she understood that while Michael didn't have much experience with football, he did have a lot of life experience protecting the people he cared about. His protection skills were strong, so when Bullock reminded him that he was good at having her back and the family's back, he could understand that he was supposed to protect the quarterback and other players just like he naturally protected his family. Once it clicked for Michael, he was unstoppable and continued to excel in football, eventually going on to play in the NFL for seven years.

Our experiences make us unique. They shape the way we see the world and are the biggest part of why we are who we are. They mold us throughout our lives like a river molds the edges of its banks. We are a born without knowing how to manage our finances, find the perfect mate, be the best friend possible, or other things like whether we should really use ketchup or mustard on our hot dog. We learn these things through experiences we share with others, things we see on TV, words we hear on the radio, education we receive, and what the people around us are saying and doing.

INNOVATIVE FUNDAMENTALS MAP APPROACH

Just like Daniel was able to get in the ring and experience victory, you too can have a simple method to practice and strengthen your skills until they become habits. Mr. Miyagi was teaching Daniel through experiential learning. I use a map as an experiential learning tool in my method. I call it *The Innovative Fundamentals Map Approach*. I chose this name because this method is about using fundamentals in innovative ways, and it also uses a map. Maps are familiar to us so they are easy to use and understand. We can visualize ourselves on the map and understand what comes next. A map creates a familiar and practical system for understanding the five steps for creating successful change. Even though the five steps of change have been basically the same for hundreds of years, I have to admit I didn't know what they were before I started studying change, and I would sometimes forget them between projects. So, while there are hundreds of thousands of books on change, the basic five steps have always been the same, and the majority of us didn't even know there is a basic five-step formula. Houston, we have a problem!

We learn how to use a map at a young age by watching cartoons like *Dora the Explorer* and seeing our parents use a GPS. The process of using a map is very similar to the five steps in the change formula. When we can visualize where we are on the map, we can figure out where we are and what we need to do next, even under the most stressful conditions. Maps are clear pictures that help keep us from getting lost. They allow us to see where we are, where we are going, and the best way to get there. We get a map out or turn on our GPS when we want to go somewhere. Using a map or GPS is particularly important when we are going somewhere new. If we are in a hurry, we may want to take the fastest route. If we like to see new things, we might want to take a route less traveled or one that is particularly scenic.

Think about this:

The first step in any change project and the first step in using a map or GPS is to decide you want to go somewhere. There is an opportunity to go somewhere new. The problem might be as simple as being hungry and the opportunity is pizza across town. The problem might also be large and overwhelming like being an alcoholic and the opportunity is getting sober to spend time with your kids. The problem might happen at work and include changing workflow for the opportunity to get a new piece of equipment. The first step in creating successful change and using a map is to identify the problem and the possibility.

The second step in any change project and the second step for using a map or GPS is to figure out where you are starting from. Our GPS does this work for us automatically, but with a map, we have to figure out where we are starting from. In change management, we call this the current state, which just means this is where you are right now. This is how things are currently. This stage is about gathering information and data to get a clear picture of the current situation. Gathering data can include: practicing mindfulness activities to get rid of distractions so you can focus on the right opportunities, writing down all of your income and expenses so you can get a clear picture of where your finances are right now, stepping on the scale to get your starting weight before starting your new diet plan, or mapping out a current process at work to get a clear picture of the process' steps or actions.

The third step in any change project and the third step for using a map or GPS is to figure out where you want to go. This is your destination or goal. Let me say this: it is possible to swap steps two and three. For example, you might have a clear idea of where you want to go before you completely understand where you are currently. There is nothing wrong with this as long as you have a clear picture of where you are now and where you want to be before you move on to the next step. If you ignore or gloss over step two and don't have a clear picture of the current problems or current state, you most likely don't have a clear picture or understanding of the real possibilities either.

These first three steps require us to organize our thoughts and information so we can see what we need to see—the problems and possibilities in front of us. These first three steps rely heavily on emotional intelligence skills found in the self-awareness and social awareness domains. These skills include the courage and self-confidence even to think about creating something new and to speak up in a group to share your thoughts and ideas. Empathy and other social skills help us to understand how others involved feel about the change and promotes good communication to find better solutions.

The fourth step in any change project and the fourth step for using a map or GPS is to figure out how you are going to get from where you are currently to where you want to be in the future. The fourth and fifth steps in any change project rely heavily on our emotional intelligence skills from the self-management and relationship-management domains. The fourth step is about planning, implementing, and testing the actions that will get you from where you are now to where you want to be in the future. It is just like choosing a route or a path—some of them have more obstacles, distractions, and detours, meaning it will take you longer to get from point A to point B, and some won't get you there at all.

The fifth step in any change project and the fifth step using a map or GPS is to figure out how to sustain your location or your success. Once you reach your destination, you are going to want to stay there as long as possible. This step relies heavily on our self-management and relationship management skills like motivation, adaptability, collaboration, conflict management, and leadership.

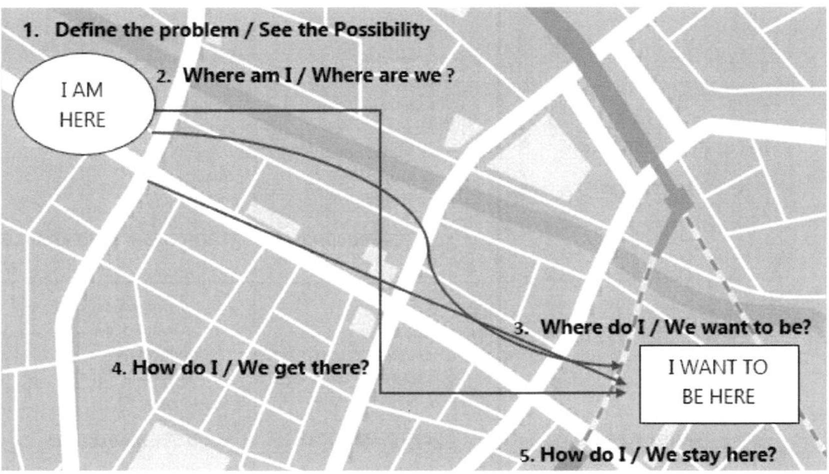

It is easier to picture yourself somewhere on your map: just starting, in progress, or sustaining improvements than it is to try to remember the five steps of change. Not knowing the five steps certainly makes creating successful change that much more difficult! We are all somewhere on the map in every area of our lives. In some areas, we are naturally successful and maintain our success in that area with ease. Other areas don't come so naturally so they require a lot of effort to keep moving forward on the correct path. Not seeing the possibilities in our lives can make us feel hopeless. Possibilities bring us hope and challenge and give us something purposeful to put our energy into. When we can align our thoughts and actions to achieve our goals, we can create successful change. Will Smith, actor, singer, husband, and father, gives this advice to his kids:

> Fail early. Fail often. Fail forward. It's always a little bit frustrating to me when people have a negative relationship with failure. Failure is a massive part of being able to be successful. You have to get comfortable with failure. You have to actually seek failure. Failure is where all the lessons are. Successful people fail a lot. They fail a whole lot more than they succeed. They extract the lessons from the failure and they use the energy and wisdom to come around to the next phase of success.

CONNECTING WHAT YOU ALREADY KNOW

We've all heard the words "connect the dots" and probably even played the game. Steve Jobs says this about connecting the dots, "You can't connect the dots looking forward; you can only connect them looking backwards. So you have to trust that the dots will somehow connect in your future. You have to trust in something—your gut, destiny, life, karma, whatever." To trust in something means to surrender to it. Oprah has talked about the moment she found out she got the part of Sofia in *The Color Purple*. She was at what she describes as a fat farm, walking around the track, crying, listening to the material around her thighs rub against each other with each step while singing, "I surrender all." She describes the agonizing four-month wait to hear any feedback from her audition. She knew deep inside that she was meant to do the part. She didn't have any experience acting in movies, but she knew she was meant to be in *The Color Purple*, just as sure as her name was Oprah. She was manifesting it into her reality with her thoughts and her actions, and when she surrendered herself at the fat farm that day, Steven Spielberg called, and as she ran from the track into the building, she didn't notice the rhythmic rub of her thighs or the voices in her head that tried to tell her she wasn't good enough. She only heard Steven Spielberg telling her she was right. She knew she was meant to play Sofia in *The Color Purple*, and even though no one else knew it yet, Oprah knew it, and she did the work.

Whether you are connecting the dots while reflecting on the past or manifesting your future by focusing on what you want to achieve, your self-awareness skills and practice of mindful activities are what help you connect with your thoughts.

CONNECTING OUR THOUGHTS AND ACTIONS

Every map has a key to help us understand how to use it. The key usually explains symbols, signs, and other information on the map so we know what the mapmakers are talking about and can, therefore, use the map. With the Innovative Fundamentals Map Approach, the key to the map shows you which skills you need for each step. You'll see below that steps 1-3 rely heavily on the self-awareness and social awareness steps. These steps are about getting our thoughts in the right place so we can see the right possibilities. Steps four and five rely heavily on self-management and relationship management and involve aligning actions with our thoughts.

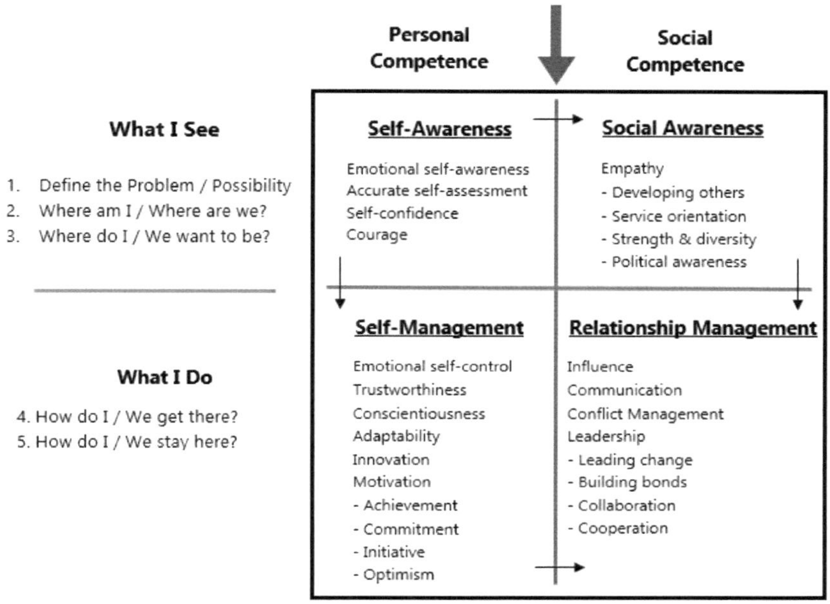

EXERCISE

Exercise Instructions:

Refresh your memory on the steps you take when you use a map or GPS. See the steps. See yourself standing in the green circle at the beginning of a journey. Think about where you are physically, mentally, and spiritually. Think about the paths on the map and how they represent the different actions you can take to reach a goal. Imagine how good it will feel to do your winning dance when you get where you want to be. Imagine how good it will feel when everyone is smiling and celebrating with you. Think about the people and things that have helped you be successful in the past. Start to think about the obvious detours, obstacles, and roadblocks you are likely to encounter.

ANSWER THESE QUESTIONS

What is going really well for me right now? Why?

What's not going well for me right now? Why?

On a scale from 1-10, with 10 being the absolute best, how do I feel about my life right now and why?

What am I most looking forward to in the future?

What are the common obstacles and roadblocks that have kept me from achieving my goals in the past?

How can I get past these obstacles and roadblocks now and in the future?

CHAPTER FOUR

LEADING...YOURSELF AND OTHERS

"Leadership is the sum total of who you are. Leaders are developed not simply born and we can all develop ourselves to be able to guide others. Anyone who follows their internal compass can become an authentic leader."

— Bill George

YOU, INC.

At a recent Pink concert in Brisbane, Australia, Pink stopped the show to give a teenage girl a hug. Leah Murphey, a fourteen-year-old from Townsville, Australia, made a sign to take to the show with her that read "My name is Leah—I'm fourteen years old. I lost my mum last month. I would LOVE a hug…Please!" As people in the audience read Leah's sign, they helped wiggle her to the front so Pink could see it. Complete strangers recognized the courage of this young lady and helped her reach her goal. Leah's mom was supposed to see Pink at that concert, but she had died before the concert date. Leah was going to go in her place, but things fell through until her aunt bought her tickets for the concert. Leah then made her sign and held it up for thousands of people to see. What kind of courage does that take? What if we could all be as courageous as Leah and hold up a sign when we are struggling, sad, or might otherwise have needs that go unnoticed? Leah, you are one of the most courageous people I have ever seen. It would have taken a lot less courage to sit at home and suffer or even go to the concert without asking for that hug. What if the people who helped Leah get to the front hadn't been paying attention? They would have missed the opportunity to support Leah in this act of courage.... And what if Pink had been so busy performing that she hadn't noticed Leah's sign? Pink is often described as the type of person who will give the world the finger one day and melt our hearts the next. But Pink did see the sign and she gave Leah the hug she wanted as everyone watched this special moment. Pink definitely melted hearts around the world at that concert in Brisbane.

Brené Brown, author of numerous *New York Times* bestsellers, including *Daring Greatly* and *Rising Strong*, says this about courage, "Courage is contagious. Every time we choose courage, we make everyone around us a little better and the world a little braver." As a research professor at the University of Houston, Brown has spent years studying the relationship between trust and vulnerability. She has found that vulnerability is the seed of trust. It is also an uncomfortable position for most people. It's considered a negative thing to feel vulnerable because it makes us look weak. Brown's research, however, revealed just the opposite—being vulnerable is a courageous act of feeling comfortable enough with yourself and the people around you that you can trust and share your authentic self.

Think about the relationships between vulnerability and trust, and friendship and trust. Today, most people are struggling to trust anyone. Can we trust that we will be safe at school? Can we trust that if we grow up to be a gymnast, actress, secretary, news anchor, or in any profession we want, that we will be safe? What about in the streets? Can we always trust the police to keep us safe? Can we trust our government will always do what's right to keep us safe? Unfortunately, most of us feel more uneasiness about our safety and security than in previous decades. So, whom can we put our trust in? We can trust in ourselves and our abilities. We can trust in the people who love us and we love back. We can trust in our faith. We can trust there is and always will be more going right in this world and in our lives than is going wrong. We can trust that we have the ability to learn about the things that impact our lives so we can connect with others to be a catalyst for the change we want to see. Maya Angelou once said, "Hope and fear cannot occupy the same space at the same time. Invite one to stay."

DERAILING

I've been watching a Netflix series called *Dirty Money*. It's a docuseries about leaders who have derailed themselves, and derailed their organizations in the process. Most of them have done so in the name of greed. One episode is about Scott Tucker, who created an illegal online payday loan business that would make high interest short-term loans to customers—mainly low-income customers who needed a little bit of money to get to the next payday. These unsuspecting customers were charged outrageous fees of all kinds and, ultimately, paid up to 800 percent for loans they couldn't even really afford. The company was automatically drafting money out of the customers' accounts, leaving them with no money to pay their car loans, house payments, or other living expenses. Meanwhile, Scott Tucker and his family were living lavishly in Aspen, Colorado, in a multi-million-dollar home. *The Aspen Daily News* reported that the Tuckers also owned five Ferraris, four Porsches, and a Learjet.

The docuseries begins in Tucker's mansion on the East Coast as his most prized possessions—his racecars—are being removed from his home, along with most of his other valuable possessions, to pay back a small portion of the money he took from his victims. His wife is speaking out about how they are taking away his babies, his cars, and how sad that is for him. She goes on say she will never buy anything seized by the government because she doesn't want to be part of any process involved in the destruction of someone's life. Tucker's various payday lending companies exploited over 4.5 million working people, which earned Tucker more than $400 million. Mrs. Tucker's diamond-covered rings were so shiny that they must have blinded her to the 4.5 million people whose lives were destroyed so she could enjoy the highest luxuries life has to offer. Yes, Mrs. Tucker, it would sure be terrible to be part of any process causing destruction to other people's lives!

Another installment of the series was about a pharmaceutical company named Valeant. CEO Michael Pearson's business approach was not to invest in research and development to create new drugs to save and/or better human lives; his approach was to increase the cost of his company's pharmaceutical products and buy several other pharmaceutical companies and raise the prices of those drugs also. Valeant bought over 110 companies and raised the cost of every medication. In 2015, Valeant raised its prices on all of its brand name drugs by 66 percent, five times more than its closest industry peer. Soon, Flucytosine, an antifungal medication, cost 10,000 percent more in the United States than in Europe. Valeant also purchased the right to two heart medications, Nitropress and Isuprel, which it immediately marked up 212 percent and 525 percent, respectively. One woman interviewed had a rare disease that required she take a pill four times a day to stay alive. With the medication, she lived a virtually normal life; without the medication, the toxins would quickly build up in her bloodstream and kill her. Once Valeant bought the company that owned this drug, the cost went from $30 a month to $20,000 a month. The woman now worries every day that she will get laid off because her healthcare costs are so expensive, and if she gets laid off, she will have a hard time finding a new job and getting insurance.

These leaders derailed. We also derail in our lives from time to time, although we probably won't see our derailment on the evening news or read about it in the newspaper. It will start out as an uneasy feeling in our gut that only we know about. The uneasiness or gut feeling is quiet at first, but as we derail further from our authentic self, the gut sense gets stronger and stronger until the inner conflict works its way out and effects all areas of our lives.

My friend Mary is a successful accountant, astutely self-aware, and one of the most disciplined people I know. She is in her mid-forties, has never been married, and has no children. She focused on her career rather than creating a family, even though that was not the norm in her culture. In fact, it is almost seen as disgraceful for children not to produce grandchildren for their parents. A few years ago, Mary was really struggling, thinking she wanted to have children. She saw doctors and gathered a lot of information about the possible options. Then one day, she told me she had decided she didn't really want to have a baby right now. She had been saving her money and living for years as if she were going to be providing for a family, but in a moment of clarity, Mary realized it was her mother who really wanted her to have a baby, and she only wanted to please her mom. Now Mary was conflicted. She realized she had taken her mom's dream of having another grandchild as her own, but after much deliberate thought and countless hours of internal conflict, Mary knew it was not the right time for her to have a baby—it might never be the right time. She also realized she loves to travel and can do that freely since she does not have any children. In the next year, she went to Costa Rica, San Francisco, New York, and several other places. She says she is very happy, and her mom is very happy for her as well.

Like the sweet, seductive Sirens that could lure sailors into the sea with their hypnotic songs, the dreams and wishes of loved ones can lure us into chasing someone else's dream. The stories say sailors would become hypnotized, unable to control themselves. The control of the Sirens was hard to resist because it was pleasurable, but when the sailors followed the seductive Sirens, they would leap out of the boat and drown. Our family's cultures and beliefs can be Siren-like as we grow up. Our goals and dreams are unique and may not match what our family and society expect of us, but they can still entice us to jump overboard and risk drowning when we don't have solid goals and dreams for ourselves. Even when we derail for good reasons, the uneasiness we feel when we aren't working toward being our most authentic selves lingers until one day we find ourselves sitting at our desks, looking around the room and wondering how the hell we got here!

LEARNING TO LEAD YOURSELF

The truth is, as with change management, most of us get very little (if any) formal or informal education on leading. In fact, leadership is almost looked at as a superpower very few possess or as the result of skills learned from an expensive college education. Neither is true. Leadership is everywhere, and leadership skills are part of the skills necessary for us to lead ourselves. Authentic leadership skills are part of the fourth and final domain of Emotional Intelligence. They are the culmination of self-awareness, self-management, and social awareness skills. Leadership skills are valuable no matter who you are, how old you are, or what position you hold.

Leaders often rise to their positions by understanding how to do the work, doing a good job, and getting promoted based on their abilities and knowledge. When they get promoted, they usually supervise people doing the job they used to do. However, doing the job you used to do and leading people who do the job are two different skill sets. John

Maxwell, author, speaker, and pastor, says, "Our ability to influence and collaborate with others directly affects how far we will go in our lives." Maxwell talks about what he calls the "leadership lid." If the leader of an organization is a four on a scale of one to ten, Maxwell says the organization will be a three because it will never rise above the lid set by leadership.

When it comes to being an authentic leader of our lives, we create leadership lids that prevent us from achieving what we are truly capable of achieving. For most of us, fear and self-doubt create the lids that hold us down! As spiritual author and life coach Iyanla Vanzant says, "If there's not something in your life that pushes you to the point where the pee is running down your leg, then you ain't living big enough." So in the words of John Maxwell and Iyanla Vanzant, if you aren't challenging yourself to reach new levels and experiencing new things, you are probably stuck on the self-imposed imaginary lid holding you back. I say, take off the lid and pee down your leg a little bit to see what you are really capable of.

LEMONADE STAND OR FORTUNE 500?

If you were the leader of an organization, as you are the leader of yourself, how would you describe your leadership style? How would you describe your organization? Is it a successful and thriving organization with a long history of success, or is it a lemonade stand or somewhere in between? We all have a leadership style that dictates how we lead our lives and how we lead others. The lemonade stand lifestyle is mostly unorganized, with some pockets of focus and success. Lemonade stands require minimal commitment, energy, time, focus, and money...you know, resources. Operating a lemonade stand is more of an occasional activity than a serious commitment.

Are you more like a startup company—a company that is newly forming? Startups have a mission and are in the process of selecting board members, establishing departments, defining roles and responsibilities, and building the organization to achieve its mission. Startup companies can be naïve at times about their levels of knowledge and knowing what to do next. Because they are doing things for the first time, they aren't going to get everything right. Mistakes will be made. However, the startups that recover from the mistakes and learn valuable lessons from them will survive. Startups require a lot of resources, particularly, time and energy because the people and processes are new and not exact or familiar yet. When a startup company makes it past the initial stage, it becomes an established company; then it is still experiencing some difficulties and unknowns, but it is also experiencing some success and growth.

Organizations with long-term success reach Fortune 500 status. These organizations have weathered the storms of change and adapted themselves, staying relevant in their environments and true to their causes. The legacy of a Fortune 500 company is related to the long-term success it has achieved, the wisdom of the fundamentals mastered over time, and the ability to adapt, collaborate, and work with well others. It consists of many successful habits that started out as processes and have been tweaked over time to create better ways of working.

You've probably never given much thought to whether you are leading your life like a lemonade stand or a Fortune 500 company. Right, I mean who thinks about themselves as an organization? That's ludicrous, or is it? What could successful people and successful organizations have in common anyway? Here are a few things:

Clear and stated purpose: We don't have to guess what Lindsey Vonn, Lebron James, or Tom Brady are passionate about. We also aren't in the dark about why many of our favorite and most successful companies exist. One of my favorite mission statements comes from Sara Blakely, the owner and founder of the wildly successful multi-billion-dollar company Spanx. Blakely was named one of *Time Magazine*'s 100 most influential people in 2012 and has long said she is serious about "making the world a better place, one butt at a time." Think about every successful person you know or have read about and every successful organization that has experienced long-lasting success. They aren't indecisive about what their goals are. They aren't hemming and hawing around, trying to decide what they are passionate about. They know what they want to achieve, and we likely know, too, because their purpose is clear.

Know their strengths and their limitations: *The Masked Singer* is a very successful new TV series on the Fox network. The singers come from all different professions and wear elaborate costumes while they sing songs to compete for the audience's vote. The singers with the most votes move on in the competition, and the singer with the least votes has to take off his or her mask. In the first season, when Terry Bradshaw, two-time Super Bowl champion and current sports newscaster, was voted off and unmasked, he was quick to admit he was going to stick to sports. He said, "Singing in front of people is much harder than playing football or newscasting." Bradshaw understands that football is one of his strengths, and he has maximized his opportunities around the game in his four-decade long career. He also understands that singing on stage in costume in front of a large audience is a weakness, and he vows never to do it again! Organizations understand their strengths and weaknesses in the same way; it's more technical and involves graphs, research, and analysis, but the knowledge of maximizing our opportunities and minimizing the threats that can come from our limitations is just good business, no matter who you are.

Don't waste their valuable resources: Resources like energy and money are not infinite, but they can be regenerated. As in, we can create more of them. Time, on the other hand, is limited and cannot be recreated. I will never get back the three hours I wasted on trying to learn the piano online, and nor will you ever get back the time you waste on things that don't really matter to you. When we waste our time on things that aren't really important to us, we take away from the time we can spend doing the things that really bring us value. For example, while I was living in England, I started watching *Keeping Up with the Kardashians*. I would catch myself binge-watching for hours. I think I probably started watching it because my sons watched it, and I kept watching it because I was missing my family and friends back in the States. Anyway, after a few months of this, I had to have a little talk with myself about the amount of time I was wasting watching the Kardashians live their lives while I was essentially wasting mine watching them. After that thought, every time I would sit down to watch the Kardashians, I would ask myself, "Is watching the Kardashians more important to me than writing my book, working out, or hanging out with friends?" Nope!

Value can be different things to different people and even different things to the same person at different times in their life. When I was a teenager, I didn't value the time I got to spend with my mother nearly as much as I do now. I don't value loud club atmospheres like I did when I was younger either, or high heels. As we get older and experience new things, we change, and some of the things we value change also. Value can be defined as the importance, worth, or usefulness of something, or as the principles or standards of behavior based on one's judgment of what is important in life. We value the people and things that are important to us, and our values, or morals as we also call them, are the standards we live by based on what and who we value.

Adapt to changes quickly: Looking forward to solutions and opportunities rather than dwelling on problems means less time wasted on "could of, should of, would of" and more time spent on "Let's find a solution." Being agile or having the ability to move quickly and easily is a key skill for any person or organization to have to continue to grow into the future and overcome setbacks, obstacles, failures, unexpected changes, and everything else that doesn't go just as planned.

Set goals and take actions to achieve them: Successful organizations create goals and actions and measure performance on them. We see them posted on the walls of our breakrooms, hear about them at company meetings, and probably earn raises and receive annual evaluations based on them. They are goals, and they direct us toward an end goal or outcome. They are the same things as dreams, but with a date and set of actions to achieve them. Successful people set goals routinely to challenge themselves. They thrive on knowing they are working toward something; in fact, we all thrive when we are working toward an achievement; it's human nature. Set a goal, any goal, and achieve it.

YOU ARE THE MOST IMPORTANT ORGANIZATION YOU WILL EVER WORK FOR

Do you work as hard for your happiness and life success as you do for the organization where you work? I have heard Oprah Winfrey quote Maya Angelou so many times that when I hear either one of them, I hear both of them. If Maya and Oprah hadn't committed themselves to their truths and purposes, despite what others and the scared voices in their heads were telling them, the world would be different, less than today. Their Olympic-size skills aren't as physically obvious as those of Shawn White, Simone Biles, or Michael Phelps because their master skills lie in the power of inspiring thoughts, understanding ourselves and others, and living with intention and purpose. They both have said there is no greater agony than bearing an untold story inside of you.

What's your story? Who are you, and what do you stand for? Every person and every organization is created for a purpose. What do you feel you were put on this earth to achieve? It can be as big or as small as you want it to be. You are the only person who can be you! No one is better at being you than you. Take some time to get to know yourself so you can really understand what makes you thrive and what holds you back.

What do you enjoy? What causes you stress? What do you want to do more of? What do you want to do less of? What do you want to learn more about? Whom do you want to spend more time with? Whom do you want to spend less time with? When are you happiest? When do you feel at your best? When do you feel your worst?

ESTABLISHING A CLEAR PURPOSE

You hear people say, "Find your purpose; live with purpose," but what does that really mean? Purpose is the reason something is done, created, or exists. It can be described as our "why," our calling, our passion, our cause, or our mission. Purpose brings meaning, excitement, growth, challenge, and happiness into our lives and motivates us to overcome obstacles and setbacks to achieve our goals and dreams. Without a clear purpose, it is easy to get lost or simply settle for mediocracy. With a clear purpose, we can reach for our full potential and create the life we would secretly love to have. Our purpose evolves over time and becomes clearer as our self-awareness skills increase and we learn more about ourselves and what is important to us. When we are actively working toward goals we are passionate about, our body rewards us and the pleasure center located in the brain is activated. Dopamine, which creates feelings of pleasure, is released into the brain. It's called getting high on life. These pleasurable feelings are addictive and motivate us to keep going even when the going gets tough. Dopamine is also increased with the use of narcotics, nicotine, gambling, and other addictive activities. Runners call it the "runner's high." Others call it "being in the zone." When we are in this state, work feels effortless, we lose track of time, and performance and creativity reach their highest levels. We see athletes, musicians, celebrities, renowned thought leaders and scholars, and a host of other very talented people who perform at the highest levels in their respected fields, and we love to watch them. We pay money, dedicate our time, and even occasionally skip work to watch them doing what they love to do. It is exhilarating to watch people doing what they love to do. But it's not just performers that we like to see living out their purpose; it's people who volunteer to serve for a bigger cause, like the gangster gardener in LA who used to terrorize the streets, but is now responsible for creating large gardens in urban areas where the community comes together to grow fresh food that is otherwise not easily attained. When he is on the news and being recognized for his work, it makes us feel good.

All of these people have a clear purpose and they can articulate it. It is clear and understood. They have a purpose statement. It's a brief statement that declares your overall goal. Organizations, clubs, and even the pool hall down the road have purpose statements. Do you already know what your purpose is? I only had a vague picture of what my purpose in life was until I was thirty-eight. I knew I was definingly put here on this earth to make a difference in the lives of others for the better. Being a nurse and nurse leader for twenty years achieved this for me. Although I have since grown and learned new and different skills, I still use the skills I learned from being a nurse and my purpose statement is still the same, but as I continue to set and achieve new goals, the way I achieve my purpose has evolved.

We will create a purpose statement in the exercise below. You may not have a very clear picture of what your purpose is right now, but no need to worry; it will become clearer as you continue to practice and develop your self-awareness skills. Right now, your purpose might just simply be to find your purpose, and today is the best time to start living your life with purpose if you're not already. In the exercise below, you will see that SAM is holding a flag. This is where our purpose statement goes; nothing states your purpose more clearly than waving a big flag with your purpose statement written on it!

SELECTING BOARD MEMBERS

Another thing successful people and successful organizations have is a trusted panel of supporters who help guide them. They may be friends, family, neighbors, coworkers, teachers, coaches, or anyone else who cares for and wants success for you. They guide us and help us make decisions just like the board members of an organization guide the organization in making decisions. Board members care about our success and support our purpose. They generally have a diverse set of skills and interests. (For example, one member may be very knowledgeable about physical fitness and healthy eating, while another may be good at finances and managing money wisely.) If Sally is a whiz at pilates, but not so great at managing her finances, let Sally be your guide to getting healthier, but choose someone else to help you get your finances where you want them. You can have as many or as few board members as you want; just surround yourself with people who love you and support you. The people on your board know you and see your blind spots (habits) when you can't. They are great resources to help us see the things we cannot see. The people you surround yourself with are great motivators, advisors, and supporters, helping you achieve your goals and dreams.

EXERCISE

You are the most important organization you will ever work for! Nobody is better at being you than you. You are important and deserve to surround yourself with people as amazing as yourself who believe in you and your purpose. Ask yourself the following questions and start thinking of yourself as the important and very successful organization you are.

Who has had the greatest influence on my life?

____

____

____

What have been the most important events in my life so far?

____

____

____

What am I most proud of?

____

____

____

What are the biggest obstacles I have overcome?

____

____

____

What do I feel most passionate and excited about?

____

____

____

What do I enjoy spending my time on?

____

____

____

What are my strengths?

____

____

____

What are my weaknesses?

____

____

____

Now take a few deep breaths and. . .imagine you are about to create the most important organization you will ever work for. You are the founder, CEO, and only employee of your organization. When your organization thrives, you thrive, and when you thrive, the people around you thrive. Commit to taking the journey to rediscover yourself, determine your purpose, and live a life of possibilities.

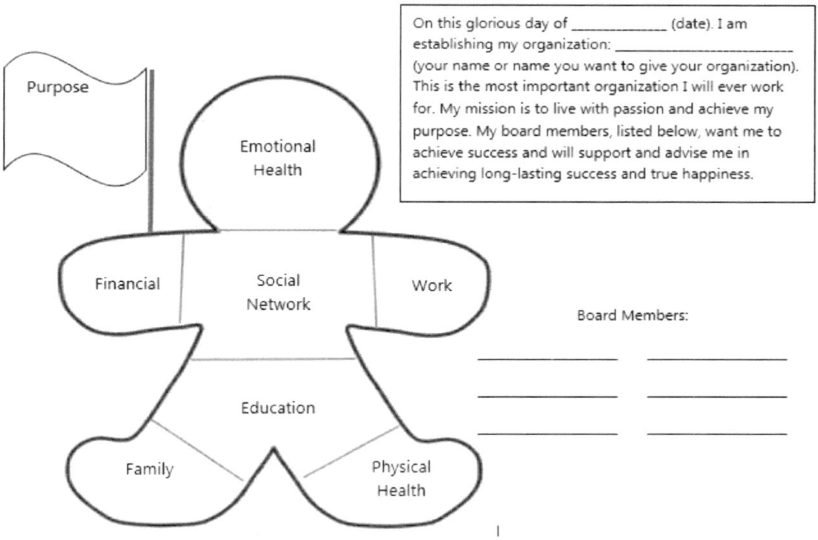

PART II

SELF-AWARENESS

CHAPTER FIVE

KNOWING WHO YOU ARE AND WHAT YOU STAND FOR

"By becoming self-aware, you gain ownership of reality; in becoming real, you become the master of both inner and outer life."

— Deepak Chopra

KNOW THYSELF

There I was, sitting on the beach in Blackpool, England, eating stringy taffy and enjoying the most impressive firework competition I had ever seen, when it hit me...not a firework, an aha moment. I don't know whether it was because of the sand between my toes, the Las Vegas style atmosphere, the smaller but still gaze-worthy Eiffel tower statue, or watching the shadows of my boys and their friends kick a soccer ball by the water's edge while the sunset colored the sky behind them. But in those moments of quiet peacefulness, I found clarity. I was new to practicing mindfulness and still half-skeptical that it could benefit me. I didn't wave sage over my head or chant mantras to the other spectators while dancing around a fire. I simply practiced being fully present in the moment. It was so pleasant that it felt hypnotic or surreal.

I wanted it to last forever.

Then, boom, out of nowhere I learned what my friends could see all along and had been trying to tell me. I had a bad habit of quickly getting into relationships and then quickly getting out of them when things didn't go well. Only this time, when I repeated my relationship cycle, I had moved to another country where the only person I knew was my soon-to-be ex-husband. As I became acutely aware of my habit that was so obvious to everyone else, I pondered the amount of time I had spent getting into and out of relationships. How many times had my sweet and very patient friends consoled me after a breakup. Then I started thinking about what I could have been doing with all of the time and energy I put into things not worth my time and energy. I had been repeating the same cycle, yet wondering why I kept ending up in the same situation. I know that is Einstein's definition of insanity, but when in the throes of a comfortable habit, I couldn't see the forest for the trees. It is always so much easier to see other people's habits than to see our own. Once I became aware of my habit, I was able to stop the insanity and create time and energy for focusing on the things valuable to me, like my family, writing this book, and helping people feel confident and courageous about change and reaching their possibilities.

I dared greatly, and I failed *greatly*! It was humiliating and terrifying. When you're 5,000 miles away from home, it's not a good time to have an all-out meltdown! I pulled it together, reminding myself that although I had made a terrible mistake, there was no sense in missing out on seeing England, Wales, Scotland, Italy, and Spain. We drove all around England in our used Volvo station wagon with 102,000 miles on it that we had bought for £1,600 pounds (equivalent to about $2,070 US dollars). One owner. Pristinely clean with a bit of a squeaky belt that always seemed to chime in when I was dropping my sons and their friends off at school. It became a running joke—the narrow street with kids in blazers, ties, gray slacks or skirts, and black dress shoes filling the sidewalks…and along comes Squeaky. We still laugh about it. We drove that car all over England without a lick of trouble from it. We hopped a train and went to Scotland, spent a long weekend in Venice, Italy, hiked the seaside cliffs in Wales, and spent a wonderful week in Spain where my boys learned how to scuba-dive. The water was clear and calm, and the moments were perfect.

I had dared greatly, failed greatly, and learned greatly. Next time, I knew I would fail better and wiser.

How well do you know yourself? There is an ancient Sioux saying, "The longest journey you will make in your life is from your head to your heart." With more opportunities at our fingertips than any generation before us, what we stand for is becoming as important as what we do. We want to know what an organization stands for before we become loyal customers. We are banding together to create movements out of what have been just moments or silent thoughts in many people's heads. From #metoo to #neveragain, individuals are working together to create the change they want to see.

Moments to movements! What do you stand for?

With so much information available, it is more important than ever before to know who we are and what we stand for. This knowledge will keep us on track for achieving our goals and dreams.

Living your life without practicing self-awareness is like setting your GPS for a long trip and then not looking at it again but still hoping you end up where you want to be. Or maybe you look at it every once in a while and then try to reroute yourself back in the right direction. If you want a smoother trip, giving yourself the best opportunity to see all of the things you want to see and to do all of the things you want to do, you are going to want to check your GPS frequently, especially when a lot of detours, obstacles, construction areas, and traffic interfere. Practicing self-awareness helps us reroute ourselves back on course in real time rather than days, weeks, months, or sometimes even years later when we are even further away from where we intended to be.

Our internal GPS communicates with us through what we often call "a gut feeling" or intuition. It's a feeling we get when things just aren't right. It is a feeling of uneasiness. Without self-awareness, we often miss the messages signaling us to reroute. We also miss the signals telling us how important this destination is. When we are clear about what is important to us, we are better able to picture our success, which keeps us motivated to stick it out through the hard times, instead of giving up with a bag of chips and tub of ice cream on the couch while binging on *Bridget Jones's Diary* movies. It reminds us what we are working toward and how good it will feel when we experience our success. Seeing our success causes our brain to release dopamine—the original and most powerful dope. It's the joy of being high on life. Dopamine makes us feel good and keeps us motivated to achieve our goals and dreams.

WHAT DO I SEE?

My dear friend Tim is one of those people who just doesn't like the Christmas holidays. He starts getting in a bad mood just after Thanksgiving and it generally lasts through January and into early spring. It doesn't matter how well things are going in his life, as soon as the Thanksgiving leftovers are gone or molding in the refrigerator, he starts getting grouchy and negative. He usually gets depressed as well. He blames his bah humbug attitude on bad experiences with Christmas as a child, although he is pretty vague about the specifics of what turned him into Scrooge. His sister, on the other hand, loves the holidays and does not have any bad memories from Christmas in their home. She has no idea what her brother is talking about.

How we see our world makes a big difference in how we experience it. Self-awareness skills are needed to look inside ourselves and know who we are and what we want to be. Social-awareness skills depend on our self-awareness skills; we can only understand others by first understanding ourselves. The first three steps of change rely on having strong self-awareness and strong social awareness. How we see things has a great deal to do with how we feel about them and the actions we take. Self-awareness activities are predominantly talked about and practiced in the areas of psychology, mental health, and mindfulness and wellbeing, but they are finding their way into mainstream education, healthcare, and many other organizations.

If you haven't taken the time to know and understand who you are and what you stand for, you don't know what's valuable to you, and you are more susceptible to peer pressure and feelings of unhappiness from leading an unfulfilled life. It's like getting in your car and driving with no idea how to get to your destination—it can be exhausting, time consuming, and defeating. Maya Angelou once said, "There is no greater agony than bearing an untold story inside you."

Through our self-awareness, we understand our strengths and limitations, allowing us to take smart risks, and grow and develop our confidence. Otherwise, fear, stress, anger, sadness, jealousy, and other negative emotions can become overwhelming and even paralyze our thinking and way of life. If we aren't aware of them, we can't manage them.

PREPARE FOR A HIJACKING

If you have ever lost your cool and let the bird fly while being unnecessarily honked at, or you have cried at a wedding, even though you swore to yourself you wouldn't, or maybe you even broke out in an all-out unstoppable laugh during a prayer at the dinner table, then you've experienced an emotional hijacking. When unmanaged emotions get out of control, an emotional hijacking occurs, sending us into Flight, Fright, or Freeze mode. When we are in this mode, or close to being in this mode, we cannot think or learn. We can only focus on what is not going well and other negative events. It can feel as though we are the ball in the pinball machine, getting bounced off every wall at lightning speed, rather than moving with purpose and control.

Emotions are a lot like change; you don't always know what they are going to be or when they will come; you can only be prepared and decide what you are going to do with them. Today, we are bombarded with more distractions and more information than ever before, yet the part of our brain in charge of our emotional wellbeing was designed thousands of years ago. (Remember your Neanderthal bodyguard.) The presence of chronic stress affects our health and wellbeing and puts us that much closer to having an emotional hijacking we will most likely regret later, once our rational brain gets a clear picture of the situation. On the other hand, positive emotions like happiness, gratitude, excitement, and joy help us focus on the positive events in our lives and allow us to see all of the possible opportunities when we are faced with a problem.

SELF-AWARENESS SKILLS

Self-awareness skills are the foundation for developing other Emotional Intelligence skills. When we understand and appreciate ourselves, we can be better at understanding and appreciating others for their strengths and weaknesses and manage ourselves and our relationships. Following are definitions of the four major self-awareness skills.

Emotional self-awareness: Being tuned into our emotions and recognizing their influence on everything we think, do, or say; using "gut sense" or internal GPS to guide our actions, behaviors, and decisions. Know thyself!

Accurate self-assessment: Knowing and understanding our strengths and limitations and recognizing opportunities and threats related to them. If you happen to be perfect, then this won't apply to you, but the rest of us have things we are really good at and things we are not very good at; we may even have some of those things listed in the wrong category. Being open to constructive feedback helps us understand where our blind spots are. We have to be aware of who we are and what we are capable of accomplishing to spark the thought that leads to the actions that lead to the journey that leads to success.

Self-confidence: A sound sense of our self-worth and capabilities. Jessie Graff, first woman to complete Stage 1 of *American Ninja Warriors*' final course said, "Everyone has limitations. I just haven't found mine yet." Will Smith says he lives a life of possibilities and that, "We should fail early, fail big, and fail often." My dad used to tell me if I haven't failed, then I haven't been trying. Are you taking smart risks? Do you know what you are really capable of achieving?

Courage: The ability to be vulnerable and risk failing in order to overcome your fears and achieve your goals. It can feel like a leap of faith when you are doing something for the first time. Courage is what gives you the strength to do it anyway, despite your fears.

CONNECTING SELF-AWARENESS SKILLS TO THE CHANGE PROCESS

Self-awareness skills are required for Steps 1-3 of creating successful change of any kind. Let's look at each of those steps to see how self-awareness skills help us be successful in each of the steps.

Step 1: Define the Problem/Opportunity (and who's going with me)

Our subconscious mind creates all kinds of stories and beliefs that can sabotage our success without our knowledge: I am not good enough; I am not smart enough; I am not pretty enough; I am not tall enough; I don't have enough money; I don't have enough time, etc. These false beliefs can sabotage our success before we even get started. Self-awareness helps us understand our thoughts and beliefs so we can sort the facts from fiction and see the real problems and opportunities.

Friends, family, significant others, or anyone else in our circle of trust can help us identify habits and tendencies that fall into our blind spots. When working with a team, it is important for all of the members to use self-awareness skills. Members who are lacking in these skills struggle to see others' points of view and often miss seeing the big picture. They are people sitting at the table who believe there is an I in team. Getting the problem right so you can see the right opportunity is the first step in achieving your possibilities. If you are busy fixing symptoms and thinking they are problems, you will find yourself very busy and very frustrated until you get to the real problem. You got ninety-nine problems? Congratulations, you also have ninety-nine opportunities!

Step 2: Where Am I/Where Are We Now (and Why)?

Self-awareness helps us to be present and understand where we are at any particular time and why. Just as a GPS has to know where we are to give us directions, tell us when we're going the wrong way, and let us know when we have arrived at our destination, our "gut sense" or intuition communicates with us. When we are creating changes to a process at work, this step is about gathering data to measure how the process works right now. If you are on a journey to lose weight and get healthy, this step might involve getting on a scale to learn your current weight and starting a journal of what you ate today. When we are working on personal growth, this step involves practicing mindful activites to reflect on the past and enjoy the present so we can be fulfilled in the future. Where we are right now is our current state—where you are right now.

Step 3: Where Do I/We Want to Be?

Self-awareness helps us understand what and who we are passionate about, gives us confidence with an understanding of our strengths, and provides valuable insight into our limitations. Self-awareness helps us know when risks are smart, and it guides us toward the things that bring us passion and fulfillment. Without some risk, we don't grow, but some risks have no value and should be avoided. Paulo Coelho once said, "When you want something, all the universe conspires in helping you achieve it." Some call it manifesting what you want. Others call it praying or meditation. Some people create vision boards to help them see what they want to create. Organizations use projections, graphs, and charts to show where they want to be, but it starts with a vision in the minds of the people creating it. Where do you want to be?

CREATING NEW AWARENESS

While I was working for a large hospital group in South Texas, I had many opportunities to reaffirm how important self-awareness can be when trying to get down to the root cause of any problem. I had unknowingly been lacking in self-awareness for most of my life until one day I realized I was tired and unfulfilled by where I had worked so hard to get. I was a superstar at bouncing back when life hadn't gone as I intended or hoped. It was one my strengths. I patted myself on the back, telling myself a lot of people would have curled up in a ball and given up if they had encountered the obstacles I had overcome. This was true, but also true was that I had created a lot of the obstacles by chasing the wrong guy, the wrong job, and the wrong dream. I didn't want to bounce back anymore; I wanted to soar to where I wanted to be, and it took becoming aware of my habits to stop them.

Old habits are like a thick and sturdy five-lane highway running through our brain that took us hours, days, months, and years to create. New habits are like a barely traveled, tiny dirt road. The good news is that little dirt roads (new neural pathways) can become major highways (established neural pathways) when they are used over and over again (thus creating habits). The highway wasn't created overnight, and it can't be torn down overnight; that is exactly why the robust process improvement tools and techniques used by successful businesses are needed for personal growth and why Emotional Intelligence is needed in organizations.

Back to South Texas. If Jonnie, one of the managers I worked with at the hospital, would have been a little more self-aware, it would have certainly made meetings more productive, created a more cohesive work environment, and most likely been the starting point to solving the problems leading to poor performance scores, high turnover, and a general lack of pride and engagement throughout the facility. You see, Jonnie had worked at the facility a long time and knew a lot about the way things worked, but she had very little control of her emotions. Her face would get beet red and her voice louder and louder until she was yelling at the slightest mention of any change that might affect her unit. Improvements happened very slowly or not at all, despite the hardships this stagnation caused for other units and their employees who were also trying to provide great patient care and reach their performance goals.

It is difficult to see the correct problem when we allow our unmanaged emotions to drive us blindly. Only when we understand what the real problem is and why it is a problem can we look for the possibility that comes with it. If we get the problem wrong, we will probably get the possibility wrong too. Maya Angelou once said, "We are as blind as we want to be."

TUNING INTO OUR INTERNAL GPS

Self-awareness is our ability to know and understand our thoughts and feelings and recognize how they influence the quality of our lives. Every word, action, and behavior begins with a thought. Self-awareness helps us form our morals and values through discovering what and who is important to us. It is our internal GPS, and although it does not speak to us in a vaguely metallic voice, telling us to reroute or that it's recalculating when we are off course, it does speak to us through our intuition or gut sense. Our brain releases chemicals into our gut that cause us to feel uneasy when our behavior is not in line with our morals or values. That uneasy gut feeling that is often unexplainable. . .like when something looks so good on paper, but just doesn't feel right...is your intuition yelling, "Reroute! Reroute!"

The opposite gut sense is also present when we are acting in alignment with our values. We get a bit of an elated or euphoric feeling in our gut we might call giddiness. Before we can be the change we want to see, we have to know what that change is. Self-awareness helps us understand what it is. Maya Angelou said, "Do the best you can until you know better. Then when you know better, do better." That's what self-awareness is, knowing yourself better so you can be better to yourself.

Remember, you are the most important organization you will ever work for. All people and organizations are created for a purpose. The goal is to take the journey of life to find out what that purpose is. Unfortunately, that goal often gets overshadowed or lost with the goals of paying the mortgage, caring for children, and climbing the ladder to pay for the roof over your head. Getting to know yourself is as easy and pleasant as a brain hug, and since life doesn't really make sense in the moment, it can only be understood in retrospect. Hindsight is twenty/twenty, and reflection is the tool we use to gain hindsight.

In my own personal life, I have noticed that since I started being mindful and reflecting daily, I can reroute myself in real time instead of years later like before. I can also motivate myself in real time and meditate to reflect on the past and see my future. It's my vision board. I envision my ultimate winning moment when I am sitting with Oprah talking about life and change. We are laughing about mistakes we've made and obstacles we've overcome. I have pictured it so many times in my head that I can actually feel the textures of the chair's green cushions and the soft wicker of the armrests. I can even smell the leaves hanging from the large oak trees in her massive yard and feel a little breeze in my hair. Self-awareness fuels our understanding of where we have been, where we are now, and where we want to go. Without it, we can work as hard as we can possibly work to climb every ladder put in front of us, but until we climb the right ladder, we will truly never reach our full capabilities.

TOOLS FOR DEVELOPING SELF-AWARENESS SKILLS

Brain Hugs (Mindful Activities)

Mindful activities are activities designed to give your brain a hug. They allow you to pause your thoughts and get into the present moment. They help you create a different relationship with the voices in your head. Meditation is the most widely used mindful activity. Regular meditation practices have been shown to improve learning, memory, emotional regulation, and sense of self. The main goal is to focus on one thought at a time. Hundreds of different ways to meditate exist. The simplest way is to focus on your breathing for two minutes and then increase the time as you get better at it. When your mind wanders, pull it back to the thing you are focusing on. Each time you do this, you improve your concentration and your ability to be in the current moment.

Meditation is not for everyone, but many other ways exist to give your brain a hug—dancing, painting, taking a walk outside, playing with your kids (two-legged or four-legged), taking time to recognize what you are grateful for, laughing with your friends, working in the yard, practicing yoga, and doing anything else that stimulates your brain so it can refresh and reset with clear thoughts and intentions. See if you can give your brain at least one hug a day for two to fifteen minutes.

5S Technique

5S is a tool used in Lean Six Sigma and other process improvement methods. It is a simple method for organizing a workspace. You can use the same method to organize your workspace, kitchen, garage, closet, and even your thoughts. Brain hugs are the way we 5S our thoughts so we can keep them organized, sorted, and ready when we need them.

Sort—Keep the items you use most often nearby and put things away that you don't use very often to reduce clutter. Practicing your self-awareness skills keeps your important thoughts readily available so you can easily access them. When we can keep our thoughts sorted, we can make sense of them.

Straighten—Establish designated spaces for the things you use often so you always know where to find them. Put fear, anger, sadness, and other negative feelings where they belong so you can understand where they are coming from.

Shine—Keep your environment and your equipment ready for use at all times. If your clock needs a battery or your lamp needs a bulb, fix it. Get rid of old, broken habits that are holding you back. Shine your thoughts up. Focus on what's going well and what you are grateful for.

Standardize—Put things back where you found them after using them and create standard processes for routine actions. Create a standard practice of self-awareness to ensure your thoughts are in the right place.

Sustain—Maintain your improvement efforts by implementing ways to monitor your success.

EXERCISES

Relax. Just do it. Yes, I said relax. Literally, give your brain a big ole, long-deserved brain hug. Think of it as going to the mental gym or spa. It is your opportunity to promote brain health; reflect on the past, enjoy the present, and think about the future; and build awareness of who you are, where you are, and where you are going.

Exercise 1

Pick at least one of the following activities and do it daily. Think of it like a sit-up—you don't get abs of steel after doing one sit-up; you develop the muscles over time with each sit-up you do. You may do the same activity every day or do a different one every day or even come up with your own mindful activity that works best for you. Incorporate the people around you when you can, whether in the office, at home, at the gym, on social media, or however you connect with others.

- Practice gratitude. What are you grateful for? Pick a time of the day to pause and think about the things you are grateful for. Say three things you are grateful for first thing in the morning before you get out of bed, or when you are in the shower. Or include your family and do it together at mealtime.
- Focus on your breathing for two minutes. Set a timer, be still, and just focus on your breathing. It sounds like it will be easy, but you'll be surprised how many times your mind wanders off. Each time it wanders off, pull your focus back to your breathing. Each time you bring your focus back, you are strengthening your ability to focus.

- Turn on a funny movie you haven't seen in a long time and laugh until you almost wet your pants.
- Call up your friends and get together.
- Turn on your favorite music and dance like nobody is watching.
- Find your inner artist. Draw, paint, dance, play, sing....
- Take a walk, run, jog, or stroll through the park.
- Get down on the floor and really play with your kids. I mean put your phone away and everything.

Exercise 2

Get organized. Clear some of the clutter out of your space: a couch that is just in the way, mail piled up on the table, an out-of-control laundry room, a full inbox, a messy sock drawer, a catch-all drawer that has caught all it can catch and has overflowed to three other drawers. Whatever it is that makes you go, "Ugh," fix it! Fix one thing that is bringing down your day, slowing down your life, disrupting your morning, stealing your peace, or ruining your fantastic day in any way. Fix it! Then sit back and enjoy your sweet success.

Exercise 3

Keep practicing your Winning Dance every day.

CHAPTER SIX

SEEING...THE POSSIBILITIES

"Change is inevitable. Growth is optional."

— John Maxwell

LEMONS TO LEMONADE TO LEMONADE STAND

You probably have never heard of Zandra Azariah Cunningham. I hadn't heard of her until I saw her on *Good Morning America* a few months ago. Cunningham is the owner and founder of Zandra Beauty, a beauty brand focused on creating natural products, a healthy skin regimen, and, for the cherry on top, a bit of daily motivation to empower other young people to look for the possibilities in front of them. At just nine years old, Cunningham began creating her first product, lip balm, when her dad refused to buy her any more. Cunningham was upset because she really loved lip balm and her dad just flat-out did not understand the importance of lip balm in her life. He refused to spend any more money on her lip balm. She tried to talk some sense into her lip-balm hating dad by explaining the importance of good lip balm and all the benefits it brings, but there was no budging Dad's decision. So Cunningham decided she'd learn how to create her own lip balm. She found that she could actually make a better product than what she had been buying. Cunningham took the lemon, turned it into lemonade, and then opened up a very successful lemonade stand out of those lemons. Cunningham is now seventeen, and recently appeared on *Good Morning America*, where her products were being showcased and some fantastic people were in the audience to get her into Sephora and some of the amazing mentorship programs available for young entrepreneurs. Way to go, Zandra!

Doors close and open all the time. If we are too busy ruminating over the door that closed, we can miss the door that is open. Open doors lead to possibilities and opportunities to learn new things and have new experiences. Closed doors are for reflecting and learning the lessons we can take from the experience as we move forward.

SEEING THE GLASS HALF FULL

If Zandra would have been stuck on seeing the glass half-empty, she would probably still be focusing on being mad at her dad for not buying her lip gloss. Instead of dwelling on the problem, she started looking for possibilities. Seeing the glass half-full, looking at the bright side of things, and remembering that every dark cloud has a silver lining are just a few ways we express what Shawn Achor calls the "Happiness Advantage." This ability to see the positive in situations primes our brain to see other positive things. The opposite is also true. In fact, it is true with just about anything you focus your attention on. Like when you get a new car and suddenly you start seeing your new car everywhere. You know you saw some cars like yours before you drove it off the lot, but now that you are paying attention, you notice a lot of cars that look like yours. Those cars didn't just apprear when you bought your new car;

they have been there all along; you just hadn't paid attention to them. The Law of Attraction is one of the most popular of the Universal Laws. It is the ability to attract into our lives what we are focusing on. The Law of Attraction is part of the science behind Shawn Achor's *The Happiness Advantage* and Rhonda Byrne's *New York Times* best-selling book, *The Secret*. People and their thoughts are both made from pure energy and the attraction of like energy to like energy attracts more of that energy into our lives.

My neighbor Mary used to sit in the office all day complaining about how there are no more good guys out there. When Mary got home, she got on the phone with her friends and continued to talk about how there were no good guys out there and how she and her coworkers talked about it all day at work. I know this because Mary and I shared a fence and she is kind of loud on the phone. Mary continued to prove herself right by telling herself all of the good guys were not available, even as she watched friends around her find good guys and go on to have happy relationships, proving her theory wrong. She continued to tell herself there were no good guys out there as she sat home on Friday nights watching *20/20* with her cats. One day, Mary met Jeff at an office party. Jeff turned out to be a super-nice guy. He had worked in the same building as Mary for about a year and had seen her before at other meetings and parties. Jeff had always thought she was pretty, but he was too shy to talk to her. Mary had been so busy being Negative Nancy that she had been missing out on being Happy Mary.

The good news is that Mary found her happiness advantage, and so can you!

SEEING WITH AN OPEN MIND

Have you ever stopped to think about how absolutely amazing it is that we are spinning on this glorious ball we call Earth out in the middle of space? We all have a one in four hundred trillion chance of being born as we are. So, in a sense, the minute we are born, we have already won the big lottery! Oprah says, "We are all put here on earth for one thing and your job is to find out what that gift is." Our parents guide us; our schools guide us; our friends, social media, movies, TV, sports figures, musicians, and politicians...all influence us; and from all of this information and experience, we determine who we are and why we are here.

We take on new experiences to find things we like to do and are good at. We don't have a tag sewn into our side stating our purpose. Our parents don't get a secret message from God or the stork announcing our purpose. We have to get to know ourselves to discover what our purpose is. There's no room for everyone to do the same thing, so everyone has a unique purpose.

I had a pretty good idea early on I should not waste my time and energy on playing the violin when my music teacher very delicately asked me, my best friend Lisa, and my sister just to move our bows with the rest of the group but not put our bows on the strings. Yeah, I wasn't good at it, and I didn't really like it either. Not like basketball, where I wanted to play and practice all the time—or gymnastics, or whatever sport I was into at any given time. When I enjoyed the sport, I was excited to practice and improve; therefore, my skills improved and I got more opportunities to play...and got better, and enjoyed it more.... You get the idea.

Enjoying what we do engages our internal reward system. It is difficult, if not impossible, to create a manufactured reward system as strong as our internal drive. Our passion fuels our internal drive and keeps us hungry and motivated to do more. The more self-aware we are, the more clearly we can see the opportunities in front of us. Trying new things allows us to experience successes and failures that build our self-confidence skills.

SEEING OUR HABITS—THE GOOD, THE BAD, AND THE UGLY

If you are a fan of the TV show, *Survivor*, then you probably remember Michaela Bradshaw. She was known for her straightforward personality and being a strong physical competitor on the *Survivor: Millennials vs. Gen X* series. She is one of my all-time favorite competitors, mainly because she grew so much from the beginning of the show to the finale. I can really relate to her. In one scene, she was trying to start a fire after everyone had given up. She wanted to give up too, but she was on a mission to start that fire. Once she got the fire lit, she jumped up and ran into the forest where she broke down in tears and fell to her knees. She had just given everything she had to light that fire, and she was overcome with joy.

But the scene that really resonated with me was when she drew the short straw and had to sit out during that week's competition, which meant she was not eligible to win the reward. Michaela was pissed. She couldn't even sit still; she was so mad that she wasn't allowed to compete. She wiggled around on the bench, lying down at times while verbalizing her discontent. While she was busy letting everyone know how unfair she felt the situation was, the camera kept panning down to a hidden advantage just under the bench where she was sitting/lying. I found myself yelling at her to look underneath the bench, but she never did. She was so busy being mad that she never saw the advantage. Sarah, who ultimately ended up winning the game and the million dollars, spotted the hidden advantage and managed to snatch it up like a ninja without anyone seeing. At the end of the show, host Jeff Probst asked Michaela about missing the advantage opportunity. In her response, you could tell she had learned the lesson and seized the opportunity to be a little bit more of the person she wanted to be.

PROBLEMS AND POSSIBILITIES

Our brains are made up of billions and billions of neurons. These neurons process up to two million bits of information per second. We really are not sure what our brains are capable of, but we have learned they are capable of a lot more than we first imagined. Scientists have found that even though our brain processes an astonishing amount of information, it doesn't forget anything it has ever seen or heard. It doesn't forget anything! This is why it's so important to make sure we are putting the right information into our memory banks. The information stored in our brains can influence us both consciously and subconsciously throughout our lives. So, while some may say ignorance is bliss, I say ignorance can also be a missed opportunity.

Before Jim Carrey made us laugh in movies like *Ace Ventura*, *The Mask*, and *Dumb and Dumber*, he was a broke and barely working, aspiring actor like so many other young dreamers. Carrey was just one of the thousands hoping to see their name up in the big lights one day. It was a dream for so many, but for him it was a problem. He had a feeling deep in his gut that he was meant to be an entertainer. He knew his ability to make others laugh was a gift and his passion.

Problems bring about feelings of uneasiness we often call our gut sense. This uneasiness is our brain communicating with us, trying to get our attention. Our thoughts are our dreams, and they are the starting point of every problem and possibility. Carrey could see the opportunity, but he didn't know how to reach it, which created the problem. Problems get a bad rap, but they can be good signs that let us know it is time to grow. It's up to us to discover what areas we want to grow in.

Carrey knew he wanted to pursue his calling to be an actor. He could see the possibilities. One night, Carey wrote himself a check for $10 million and put "for acting services rendered" on the memo line. He dated it for two years in the future. He carried this check in his wallet and looked at it frequently. Carrey had no idea how he would make the $10 million. He just knew he would. Some people call this manifesting what you want. Manifestation is the ability to perceive something in our senses, primarily in our sight, and let the Universe know we are aspiring to achieve it. Some might also call it a self-fulfilling prophecy, where the effects of behavior confirmation influenced by expectations cause those expectations to come true. When Carrey wrote himself that $10 million check, he was influencing his behavior by setting a clear expectation of earning $10 million within two years.

I have a friend who writes down her intentions on a piece of paper and stuffs the paper in her bra. Another friend writes her intentions on a piece of paper and puts it inside a silver box in the corner of her bedroom. My friend Jim always has his written on the big white board in his office. In business, we call this forecasting or projecting. Whatever you call it, and however you do it, it's all based on self-awareness skills: the ability to know who you are, what you stand for, and where you want to go. When you can get clear about what and who is important to you, you can also get clear about the possibilities out there. Groups with higher levels of self-awareness are better able to work together to find the real problems and possibilities in the boardroom, the classroom, the community, on the soccer field, and everywhere people work together.

WHY, BABY, WHY?

"Why?" is one of the most important questions we can ask ourselves and others. "Why?" is so important that Simon Sinek wrote a book titled, *Start With Why*. The book was an instant *New York Times* bestseller and gets at the core at how much our "why" drives every aspect of our lives—sometimes without us even being aware of it. I know a very sweet lady who was in the massive tornado that went through Wichita Falls, Texas, in 1979. This large storm caused massive devastation and some loss of life. All of this helps me understand why, to this day, this woman starts heading toward her cellar when there's barely even hints of a storm on the way. We all have a *why* that guides everything that comes next. In the business world, why is an important question too, particularly when trying to get to the root cause of a problem. One of the most popular tools for getting to the core of why something is occurring is asking the question "Why?" to find out why something is working well. It can be just as important as asking it when things aren't going well. The 5 Whys technique is used to explore the cause-and-effect relationships of a particular problem. This technique helps get down to the root cause of the problem by asking the key question, *why*, until you get down to the real reason the problem exists. The technique is quite simple. Each answer forms the basis of the next question. Five is the number of times needed to get to the root of the problem. The 5 Whys technique can also help us identify the root of possibilities in the same way it identifies the root of problems. Asking ourselves why we value something can help us understand the roots of our values and morals.

Here's a 5 Why example about the Washington Monument:

Problem statement: The Washington Monument, one of our capital's most iconic structures and its tallest, is deteriorating.

Why 1: Why is the Washington Monument deteriorating?

- The use of harsh chemicals on the surface.

Why 2: Why do we use harsh chemicals on the surface?

- To clean up after the pigeons.

Why 3: Why are there so many pigeons?

- Pigeons eat spiders and there a lot of spiders here.

Why 4: Why are there so many spiders here?

- Spiders eat gnats and there are a lot of gnats here.

Why 5: Why are there so many gnats here?

- Gnats are attracted to the display lights at dusk.

Root of the problem: The lights coming on at dusk attract gnats.

Solution: Program the lights to come on after dusk so the gnats won't swarm the lights and attract the spiders, which ultimately attract the pigeons that poop on the Washington Monument.

STEP 1: DEFINE THE PROBLEM/SEE THE POSSIBILITY

The first step in creating successful change is to identify the correct problem or problems so you can see the right possibilities. If you have ever worked really hard to achieve something only to find out it wasn't actually what you wanted, you probably got the problem wrong to begin with (and you're not alone!). Your self-awareness skills will help you get to know yourself better so you can identify the things in your life that are really causing you pain, stress, grief, or general dissatisfaction. Endless possibilities are in front of you; you just may not be able to see them yet. Be patient and get to know yourself; you are worth it!

EXERCISES

Seeing the possibilities often requires seeing the problems first. Remember, problems aren't bad; they are life's way of telling us it's time to grow. Defining the problem and seeing the possibility require gathering as much information, data, and insight as you can related to the project you are working on. Project experts make a large project more manageable by breaking it down into more manageable pieces. Remember, organizations do this by creating different departments. We can do this by thinking of the seven keys areas of life important for our success and happiness.

TOOLS FOR DEFINING THE PROBLEM AND SEEING THE POSSIBLIITIES

Brainstorming:

Brainstorming is a process for generating creative ideas and solutions. It is usually done in small groups and involves open discussion of thoughts and ideas. Individuals can use the same process to brainstorm their own thoughts and feelings. Keep in mind that we can't see our blind spots, but the people close to us can give us insight into those habits and tendencies. Once we practice brainstorming and get comfortable with it, we feel more comfortable seeking insight from others.

Rules for Brainstorming:

- Set a time limit for brainstorming.
- Let thoughts and ideas roll freely.
- Do not judge any ideas or thoughts.
- Record all brainstorming ideas and thoughts (sticky notes or paper).

When the brainstorming time has ended, capture the responses and evaluate the information you have recorded.

Affinity Diagram:

An Affinity Diagram is a way to organize information gathered from brainstorming. It involves clustering thoughts and ideas into groups with similar ideas. Sorting thoughts and ideas brings clarity and focus and helps develop self-awareness. Cluster sticky notes into groups and determine how they fit into your organization. They will all most likely fit into one of your seven fundamental areas of life and your purpose for that area, and they will give you some information about where you are and where you want to go.

SWOT Analysis—Strengths, Weaknesses, Opportunities, and Threats

A SWOT Analysis is a form of brainstorming used to identify an organization's strengths, weaknesses, opportunities, and threats. It involves evaluating and sorting brainstorming information into groups based on whether the information is seen as a strength, weakness, opportunity, or threat.

- **Strengths:** Characteristics of the organization that give it an advantage over others.
- **Weaknesses:** Characteristics of the organization that place it at a disadvantage relative to others.
- **Opportunities:** Elements in the environment that the organization could use to its advantage.
- **Threats:** Elements in the environment that could cause trouble for the organization.

Strong relations between strengths and opportunities could provide the perfect opportunity to find passion and purpose. Strong interactions between weaknesses and threats could be a sign of potential danger.

EXERCISE 1

Perform a brainstorming exercise described above using this question: What is going on in my life right now that is keeping me up at night and causing me some stress, sadness, or grief? Use sticky notes for the exercise. Write down everything that comes to mind on a separate sticky note.

EXERCISE 2

Create an Affinity diagram described above with the sticky notes from your brainstorming exercise. Group the sticky notes into like groups and see what common themes emerge.

EXERCISE 3

5 Whys Technique Exercise: From Exercise 2 above, select one of the things causing you grief in your life right now and list it in the problem statement below.

Problem statement: ______________________ is causing me stress, sadness, pain, or general unhappiness and is holding me back from achieving the best version of myself.

Why 1: Why is ______________________________ happening?

Answer 1: ____

Why 2: Why is (Answer 1) ______________________ happening?

Answer 2: ____

Why 3: Why is (Answer 2) ______________________ happening?

Answer 3: ____

Why 4: Why is (Answer 3) ______________________ happening?

Answer 4: ____

Why 5: Why is (Answer 4) ______________________ happening?

Answer, **Root of the problem:** ____________________________

Solution: ____

____

____

It will take a little practice to feel comfortable using these tools, but the more you practice them, the more skilled you will become at asking why.

EXERCISE 4

Use the tools above to answer the questions below related to the Innovative Fundamentals Seven Areas of Life. Think about the areas of your life that help you thrive. Think of the different ways they serve you in achieving your overall purpose. Remember, areas that perform poorly are hindering you from achieving success, and areas that perform well are helping you achieve success. The goals and functions of each area must be aligned and work together to achieve your overall purpose.

Work (Job/Career/Calling)—A job is a paid position of regular employment. A career is an occupation undertaken for a significant period with opportunities for advancement. A calling is a strong urge toward a particular way of life—a vocation. None of these is about the amount of pay or the title—they are all about the way you feel about what you are doing and your commitment to it.

How do I feel about the work I am doing?

____

How do I feel after a day at work—fulfilled, exhausted, stressed, inspired?

____

Do I have a job, career, or calling?

____

Financial—Money, cheddar, lettuce, green, bucks, bread, scratch, bones, or dough…whatever you want to call money, managing how you make it, spend it, and save it is likely one of the most stressful parts of your life.

How do I feel about my financial situation?

____

Do I have a system for managing my finances?

____

Do I generally experience success or failure with managing my finances?

____

Family—Our families influence all areas of our lives. They shape our morals, values, and beliefs during our most formative years.

How has my family influenced my life in positive ways?

____

Has my family influenced my life in negative ways? If yes, then how?

____

Have I picked up any bad habits from my family? What are they?

____

Among my family, who has inspired me the most?

____

Physical Health—The cost of stress on our bodies is significant, so learning to manage stress effectively can dramatically improve our physical health. Without good physical health, it is hard to achieve success. Our health provides us with the opportunities to experience life.

How do I feel about my physical health? (Circle Answer)

Confident, not so confident, scared?

What is affecting my health negatively right now?

____

What things are impacting my health positively right now?

____

Education—Education includes spending time learning and experiencing new things. It can be formal or informal.

What new things have I been wanting to learn about?

____

What is holding me back from learning them?

____

What is the last learning experience I really enjoyed?

____

Social Network—Having supportive, loving relationships is vital to our wellbeing. We all have a sense of longing to feel like we belong, we are valued, and we are connected with others. Who we spend our time with greatly affects the quality of our lives and the choices we make.

Who are the five people I spend the most time with?

___

Who are the people in my life who have achieved the things I want to achieve?

___

How often do I get together to laugh and share with friends?

___

Emotional Health—Our emotional health is vital to our success in every aspect of life. Our emotions influence everything we think, do, and say. They move us to action, and if we don't manage them, they will control us. Staying aware of our emotions allows us to keep negative emotions like fear, anger, jealousy, and sadness from hijacking our goals, dreams, and happiness.

Use three words to describe how I feel right now:

___

Use three words to describe how I want to feel:

___

CHAPTER SEVEN

MEASURING...WHERE AM I NOW?

"Peace of mind always comes with knowing who you truly are, where you currently stand, where you positively need to be, and strongly believing in its possibility."

— Edmond Mbiaka

THE CHICKEN OR THE EGG?

Success—what is it really? We all know we want it. We are raised to achieve it. But what does it mean to be successful? Is it having a big pile of money, a job that pays a great salary, the biggest house in the neighborhood, a big family? Whatever success is to you, you probably were raised to believe that once you achieve it, you will be happy.

Once I achieve success, I will be happy.

We have certainly seen that myth proven false as we have witnessed numerous intentional and accidental deaths of celebrities, icons, and legends over the past few years. Highly successful individuals at the top of their respective industries like Michael Jackson, Prince, Kate Spade, and Robin Williams remind us we are all ordinary when it comes to managing our insecurities, self-doubt, depression, and fear.

When Shawn Achor studied success and happiness at Harvard, he found a bit of a chicken and egg story. Which came first? Achor's research found that happiness comes first, and actually, is part of what inspires the success. In fact, he defines happiness as, "The joy you feel when working toward a goal." If you think about it, once we achieve a goal and celebrate our success, we generally set another goal to achieve. We are designed to grow and evolve, and we are in our happiest state when we are doing just that.

Money has been considered an important measure of success for many years. To a large extent, it is still seen as the top indicator of success for individuals and organizations. However, the bigger, better, faster lifestyle we have all become so accustomed to is starting to lose a little of its appeal as we start to redefine what success looks like. The simplicity of just being and the negative effects of stress, sleep deprivation, high blood pressure, unhealthy diets, social media, etc., have created an awakening. People are now asking themselves questions about what really makes them happy.

WHAT GETS MEASURED IMPROVES

We love to measure things. We measure all kinds of things, but are we measuring the things that really matter to us? Are we measuring the right things? It has been said, "You can't improve what you can't measure," which makes some of the more intangible things like emotional intelligence, happiness, and empathy more difficult to measure than more tangible things like how fast you can run a 100-yard dash or how many marshmallows you can fit in your mouth. Intangible things are unable to be touched or grasped and have no physical presence. This makes them very hard to measure and track. We can make something more tangible by visualizing and connecting the intangible with a familiar experience (experiential learning). Much like a dog wagging its tail is a universal sign of happiness in dogs, the smile is the universal sign for happiness. The smile and the tail wag are both tangible expressions of intangible feelings.

In schools, we measure academic achievement with tests like STARR and others. The entire school curriculum is developed around these tests. The lessons are taught to the tests. Schools get funding based on the test scores…but these test scores do not really measure how successful a child will be; they only get them in the door to their next level of education.

The IQ ranking on these tests has been determined to be responsible for less than 10 percent of a student's success in college and life. Most schools list desired core characteristics of their students in their hallways and on their websites. Desired characteristics include leadership, trustworthiness, commitment, and adaptability, all of which happen to be EQ skills, which some schools teach as Social and Emotional Learning (SEL). Some talk has arisen of pushing SEL as a national education standard, but it is not currently taught in the overwhelming majority of US schools. Schools that teach SEL experience an increase in academic performance and a decrease in absenteeism and disruptive behaviors. Schools that include emotional intelligence training for staff experience the same benefits as seen in the students. The staff feels better. They are more engaged with work. They are working in a thriving environment and can get excited about the work they do. In this case, the staff also shows a decrease in absenteeism and disruptive behaviors, and performance and productivity increase.

Ask yourself these two questions to help you measure the right things:

1. What is my objective or purpose?
2. What factors will help me achieve that objective?

BE CAREFUL WHAT YOU MEASURE (WISH) FOR

Albert Einstein once said, "Everybody is a genius. But if you judge a fish by its ability to climb a tree, it will live its whole life believing it is stupid." While most of us aren't spending our days judging fish climbing trees, we are most likely working in environments where things are being measured. Some of these measures you track for your boss are probably as beneficial as judging the fish climbing the tree, but others are very valuable. Gross Domestic Product (GDP) is a measure of the value of all goods and services produced by a country. It is perhaps the single most powerful statistical indicator in history and has a huge influence on global policy. The GDP is so important because it is considered a measure of the economy's size and includes all consumption by households, all investment by businesses, all purchases by the government, and all exported goods minus all imported goods. In other words, everything we buy—food, cars, houses, bicycles, diapers—is included along with all of the services we use: internet, cable, mani-pedis, attorney fees, healthcare services, etc. It includes everything the government purchases from fighter jets to desks and all of the investments made by businesses. If the GDP increases, it is a sign of good things happening or about to happen like people getting more jobs and businesses feeling more comfortable with investing. You may be looking at this like me and thinking, hmm...are we really measuring the right thing? In fact, you wouldn't be alone in asking that question! As far back as 1968, Bobby Kennedy said this about the GDP, "It measures everything in short, except that which makes life worthwhile." Just in case you were wondering, the United States has been ranked number one in GDP for many years.

Other forms of measurement are out there, like the Social Progress Index (SPI) proposed by the Social Progress Imperative organization led by Harvard Economist Michael Porter. The organization states that the

SPI is a good companion to the GDP because it shows the relationship between economics and social progress. The group studied fifty-four distinct indicators of wellbeing and came away with three key measures: 1) Does a country provide for its people's most essential needs? 2) Are the building blocks in place for individuals and communities to enhance and sustain wellbeing? 3) Is there opportunity for all individuals to reach their full potential? The United States scores high (fifth in the world) in providing opportunity, but relatively low (twenty-third) in providing basic human needs. The SPI is thought to be a good predictor because it looks at the relationship between economics and social wellbeing.

When we look at just GDP, and leave out SPI, we have no room for improvement. And, unfortunately, we get situations like the United States spending more on healthcare than any other country (a GDP measure), yet performing very poorly in the area of life expectancy (an SPI measure)—thirty-first at the time of this writing, just above Cuba and right after Chile and Costa Rica.

If we are measuring the wrong thing, the right opportunities can't be found. Resources will be wasted on things that do not add to the process or outcome's value.

I AM HERE

Mark Cuban, self-made billionaire, owner of the Dallas Mavericks, and shark on TV's *Shark Tank*, said, "If you don't know your numbers, you are going bankrupt and don't know it yet." Dan Buettner, author of *The Blue Zone*, said, "If you can't measure it, you can't manage it."

Understanding where you are starting from can be as simple as stepping on the scale to see what your starting weight is before going on a new diet or as complicated as understanding Mark Cuban's combined balance sheet from all of his companies. Whatever it is, if you can measure a beginning point, you can measure progress and success along the way until you reach the end point. Reflecting gives our brains time to process all the information taken in to understand our thoughts. Reflection provides the deeper understanding and appreciation that comes from building our self-awareness skills and realizing or discovering what is valuable to us. An accurate self-assessment can provide all of the information we need to know about ourselves to understand what we value and why we behave and act the way we do. It's a deeper understanding of what we value and why we value it.

Are you measuring the right things in your life? If you are measuring the number of friends you have on social media, the size of your house, or your bank account, and find you don't feel fulfilled, maybe those aren't the things you really value.

The leaders of successful organizations meet frequently (often daily) to discuss how they are performing. They often use quick reports called dashboards because you can look at the report just like you would look at the dashboard of your car and immediately get most of the information you need to maintain and operate the vehicle safely and successfully. If there is about to be trouble, you will get a warning, like a yellow blinking light. If there is already trouble, you get an alarm, like a red light or loud beeping noise. Dashboard reports give us a lot of information quickly and efficiently.

I'M A 10

Self-awareness is about understanding yourself. While we don't generally use dashboards of any kind in our personal lives, we don't generally have a lot of success in balancing our lives and achieving overwhelming success either. Using a simple dashboard-type report can help us keep track of and measure our progress in the seven key areas of our life. It's easy to get out of balance with responsibilities and obligations if you don't have a tool or system you use regularly to track your progress Remember what Mark

Cuban said about knowing your numbers? While he was talking about knowing the numbers for your business in terms of dollars, projections in sales, performance, production, and other numbers to track how well your organization is performing, imagine if we kept track of our performance in the seven key areas of our lives in real time, like Mark Cuban. And imagine if we could manage our time, money, and resources with intention and focus on achieving our goals, whatever they might be.

The simple dashboard report I created for us to use in our personal lives is called "I'm a 10." This scoring system is designed to help us determine how we feel we are performing in each of our key areas so that we can keep in balance and moving toward achieving our goals. Who doesn't want to be a 10 in their own life? Each of the seven areas is valued at one point and your purpose is valued at three points to equal a maximum of ten points. Each area is measured by how you feel you are performing based on what is important to you. Areas in which you score high are those in which you are performing well and that are helping you achieve success in reaching your goals. Areas in which you score low are areas in which you are performing poorly and that are hindering you from achieving the success you desire. The rating system creates an easy way to assess how you think about how you are performing in each of your seven areas and why you feel that way. When you record your score for each of the areas and total them, write your total score in the "I Am Here" box. This is your starting point or baseline data: it's where you are now. Just like stepping on the scale shows you what your weight is right now. See the diagram for "I'm a 10" below.

SCORING FOR I'M A 10

Excellent: Success in this area occurs very often. This area is regularly focused on, and rarely neglected or met with failure.

Above average: Success in this area occurs often. This area is often focused on, but sometimes neglected or met with failure.

Average: Success in this area occurs sometimes, perhaps more often than not. This area is sometimes neglected, sometimes focused on, and met with a mixture of failure and success.

Below average: Success in this area occurs occasionally, but not most of the time. This area is neglected or met with failure regularly.

Well below average: Success in this area very rarely occurs. This area may be completely neglected or met with failure most of the time or often, for whatever reason.

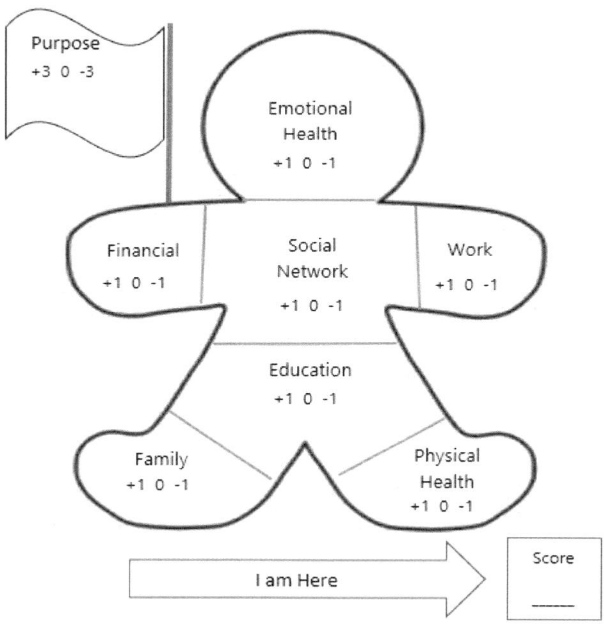

STEP 2: WHERE AM I/WHERE ARE WE?

The second step in creating successful change is to figure out where you are starting from. Understanding who you are and what you stand for forms your morals and values and this is the absolute best place to start any decision, action, journey, or thought from. When we take action without first considering our morals, values, or purpose, we risk derailing ourselves from achieving what we want to achieve. and helps you to discover your purpose so that you can get passionate about spending more time and energy on the things you are truly passionate about rather than on things that are habits or comfortable distractions. Where you think you are starting from and where you are actually starting from is the difference between assuming you are living the life you really want and knowing you are absolutely living the life you really want. Remember purpose isn't something you create or buy at a store, it's a gift you already possess that has to be discovered first, then developed. You have to sift through the daily grind, comfortable distractions, and unknown habits to get to know yourself. You are so worth it!

TOOLS FOR DEVELOPING SELF-AWARENESS SKILLS

Trend Analysis

Trend analysis is collecting information and attempting to spot a pattern, or *trend*, in it. For example, I noticed when I go to yoga that I feel calmer and more relaxed. I also noticed when I go out with friends on Thursday night, I am often late to work on Friday. Anything can be trended: our weight, spending, mood. Do you ever stop to think when you are at your happiest, saddest, most frustrated, bored, or excited? What are you doing at that particular time? Recognizing our patterns is helpful for seeing our blind spots, which is where our good and bad habits live. Remember, recognizing the habits that make us successful is just as important as recognizing the ones that hold us back.

Spaghetti Diagram

A *spaghetti diagram* is a visual representation using a continuous flow line tracing the path of actions throughout a process. The continuous flow line enables us to identify redundancies in work flow and opportunities to evaluate what we are spending our time on and why.

Process Mapping

Process mapping is a visual depiction of a process' steps or actions. Mapping the individual steps or actions of a process helps us understand it. I have so many stories about what has gone wrong when people assume they know how a process works. Here is one of my favorites to help remind you how important it is not to assume you know how a process is actually working:

My good friend Sandy was teaching her young son to wipe the toilet off when he's done peeing. She showed him a few times with toilet paper, and after four or five days, she noticed he was regularly wiping off the toilet. Sandy is very particular about her skin care regimen and washes her face every morning and night without fail. In the morning, she uses a clean washcloth, then hangs it to the side to dry until the evening, when she uses it again before putting it into the wash. Sandy was pleased her son was consistently wiping down the toilet. One day, however, she happened to walk by as he was doing it—with her washcloth. When she asked him about it, he said he had been using washcloths for months because one was always hanging there by the sink. Sandy had assumed she understood how the process was working, just like many of us assume we know how the processes in our lives are working, and in the same way managers think they know how the processes in their departments are working. Improvements made in steps or actions improve the process and the end result. Remember, better thoughts create better actions, and better actions create better processes.

Once you map out the steps within a process, you can better understand the entire process. If you want to improve the process to get better results from it, mapping out the steps helps to know which steps can be cut from the process to improve it. Some steps within the process add value to it, while other steps don't add any value. Value is not just monetary value, although that might be a benefit of improving a process. Value is the benefit, both internal and external, that results from the action. For example, I enjoy spending time with my mother, but there is no monetary value in spending time with her. The value is in our connection and love for each other. What you value may be different from what others around you value because everyone is a little different in experiences and beliefs. Value-added steps are good. The more you have in any process, the more efficient you are—leading to less wasted time, energy, and money.

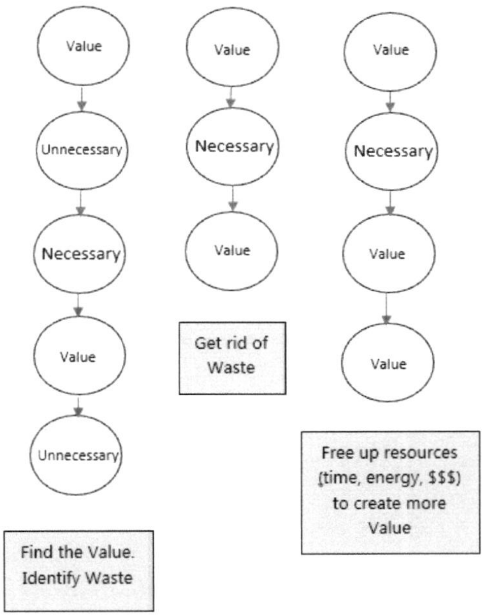

Some steps don't add value, but they are necessary; some steps add no value and are not necessary. The steps that add no value and are unnecessary can be eliminated from the process to improve it. This is a good way to manage time, energy, and money so the things that really matter to you are achieved.

Here's a summary of various types of steps and how they add or don't add value:

Value Added—These steps or actions are necessary and add value to the process or end result. If you are mapping out the process of boiling water, putting water into some kind of heat-resistant container is necessary for the process and adds value. Without the container for the water, the end result would not be possible. Think of these value steps as a green light. Green for go.

Non-Value Added and Necessary—These steps add no value but are necessary to complete the process, like waiting for water to boil. The waiting time does not bring any value to the process, but it is necessary for the end result. Think of these steps as a yellow light. Proceed with caution, slow down, and evaluate these steps.

Non-Value Added and Unnecessary—These steps add no value to the process or end result and are not required to complete the process. Let's say while you are waiting on the water to boil, you slip into the pantry and grab a handful of Mint Oreos to pass the time. Although the Oreos are very good, they do not add any value to the process and are not necessary. Think of these steps as red lights. Red means stop. Stop wasting your time, energy, and other resources.

EXERCISES

EXERCISE: I'M A 10

In the exercise below, rate each of your seven areas from +1 for excellent to -1 for well below average. Then rate how well you are doing at living your life with purpose. Give yourself a +3 if you are succeeding at living with purpose and a -3 if you don't have any idea what your purpose is. Record your score for each area and write your total score in the "I Am Here" box.

SCORING FOR I'M A 10

Excellent: Success in this area occurs very often. This area is regularly focused on, and rarely neglected or met with failure.

Above average: Success in this area occurs often. This area is often focused on, but sometimes neglected or met with failure.

Average: Success in this area occurs sometimes, perhaps more often than not. This area is sometimes neglected, sometimes focused on, and met with a mixture of failure and success.

Below average: Success in this area occurs occasionally, but not most of the time. This area is neglected or met with failure regularly.

Well below average: Success in this area very rarely occurs. This area may be completely neglected or met with failure most of the time or often, for whatever reason.

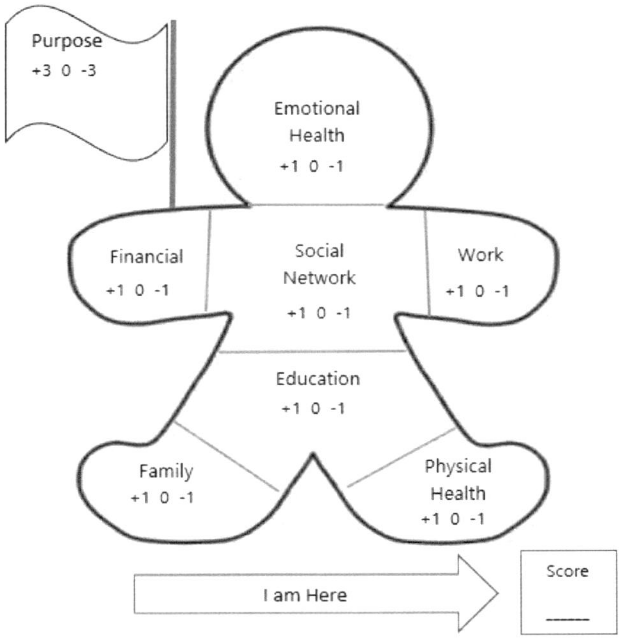

CHAPTER 8

FOCUSING ON WHAT YOU WANT

"When you want something, all the universe conspires in helping you achieve it."

— Paulo Coelho

KEEPING YOUR EYE ON THE PRIZE

Have you ever written down a goal and posted it on your bathroom mirror, or maybe created a vision board, or written down a goal and stuffed it in your bra, or envisioned yourself celebrating with your winning dance? My spiritually-inclined friends call this process raising your energy to manifest what you want. Whatever you call it—manifesting, forecasting, projecting, or just goal-setting—it's an important part of success. Focus is the opposite of distraction, and our daily lives consist of far more distractions now than ever before. In fact, virtually every area of our lives is affected by distractions. A $13 billion pharmaceutical industry is related to our inability and/or unwillingness to focus. We even have cars that prevent us from veering into the next lane when we are distracted. For the really distracted, an alarm will remind us not to leave our children in the car.

Matthew McConaughey is well-known for one word repeated three times: "Alright, Alright, Alright." You may remember it from the movie *Dazed and Confused*. In an interview, McConaughey revealed the story behind his famous line. It was his first role in a major film. He was nervous and didn't really have much information on his character when the director decided to shoot his scene first. Rather than freak out, he thought about what he did know. He knew three things about his character, so he offered affirmations and expressed gratitude for those three things, saying, "Alright, alright, alright," and the director loved it enough to keep the lines in the film.

Our brains are geared to help us survive. One amazing thing they do is secrete chemicals that bring us pleasure and guidance to keep us feeling motivated and alive. Dopamine is one of those feel-good chemicals. Dopamine produces feelings of happiness, alertness, and focus—just like drugs made by the pharmaceutical companies and some street drugs. Our bodies crave dopamine. When we are working toward a goal, thinking about how awesome it is going to feel when we succeed at the end is what keeps us motivated to keep going despite obstacles, roadblocks, detours, and life in general. Dopamine motivates us to persevere. Internal motivators like dopamine are the most powerful motivators there are. Our bodies crave dopamine, so if we aren't getting it internally, we will search for it externally, through drugs, alcohol, relationships, and even our cellphones. The sound of our phone going bing, ding, or ring elicits a dopamine response that has been found to be just as addictive as drugs, alcohol, or gambling.

Here's a chicken or the egg situation to think about. Do we have to see it to believe it, or believe it to see it? Roger Bannister was the first person to run a mile in under four minutes. Everyone said it could not be done, but Bannister felt like they were wrong. He said, "As it became clear that somebody was going to do it, I felt that I would prefer it to be me." He envisioned himself running a mile in less than four minutes. He trained his body relentlessly and trained his mind also. Because Bannister was able to believe it, the world was able to see it.

Whichever it is, believing first or seeing first, the dopamine reaction to focusing your thoughts, energy, and time on what you want motivates you to continue. It puts you into the zone or in flow.

THE LOST ART OF FOCUS

It would be hard to argue that our ability to focus is *not* going by the wayside. Distractions have become common, and the latest technology and inventions keep creating new ways for us to avoid paying attention. The amount of information we encounter every day is phenomenally more than encountered by previous generations. Our minds have to filter through this massive dump of information to figure out what is important, what is meaningful, and what is real. Trying to sift through all of the distractions to figure out who you are and what you stand for is more important than ever. Those who are not tuned into their own thoughts, beliefs, and values can find themselves heavily influenced by peer pressure and living out someone else's dreams rather than your own. Focusing on your connection with your thoughts and beliefs keeps you tuned into your internal GPS so you can recognize when you are on your best path and when you are on the wrong path. Our internal GPS works just like the GPS on our phone. Without knowing where you are starting from and where you are going, you are really just sitting there looking at a blank screen wondering which way to go.

Our internal GPS doesn't shout at us through a speaker to tell us we need to reroute or recalculate. It releases a chemical from our brain into our stomach to produce our gut sense. It's an uneasy feeling that's hard to describe; it may feel like hesitation or doubt. Our internal GPS sends us messages throughout the day that we can easily miss if we are not tuning into what's going on in our heads. Here's what's happening: Our brains are bombarded with more information in an ordinary day than they can fully process. We tune out a lot of the information coming in. Distractions keep our thoughts on the superficial level where they can be scattered and are not well grounded. Stopping to be mindful allows our brains time to catch up and sync up with the rest of us, so our thoughts, actions, and behaviors can align. For a long time, I was so distracted that my life really had a life of its own. Underneath my crazy, chaotic, fast life—which most of the time I was loving—was a calm, peaceful place that had been there all along, and I didn't know it. When I found this peaceful place, it was like finding the most spectacularly beautiful, magical place I had ever been.

I was lying on my son's bed waiting for the shower when we lived in England, something that never would have happened in the United States because: 1) we generally always had the convenience of having multiple showers to choose from in the house so we really didn't have to wait, 2) we always had the luxury of having TVs in all the bedrooms, and 3) I was fortunate enough always to have friends to talk to when I had a moment of free time. But in England, we had one shower, a quiet room with no TV, and a six-hour time difference from all my friends and family in the States, which made it impossible to talk to them whenever I wanted or needed to. I lied down on the bed with only the sunshine coming in from the window. Yes, sunshine in England. Lying there felt so good—my breath was the only noise I could hear. It was peaceful.... My mind was at rest and so was my body, and it felt spectacular.

When I found this peaceful place, I felt the chaos drifting away. When I was able to stop and just breathe, which then turned into the ability to stop, breathe, and focus, I was able to filter out all the things that really weren't valuable to me and move that energy, time, and money toward the things that *are* important to me. You most likely have things you are doing right now in your life that are distracting you from your full awesomeness. These little time-wasters don't really add any value to our lives; they are just habits we take on and get comfortable with. When we focus on distractions instead of the things that add value to our lives, we end up having to rely more on our discipline muscles. Research indicates we can only really make about twenty good decisions in a day before decision fatigue sets in. Decision fatigue is the deteriorating quality of our decisions after a long period of decision making. When we get mentally fatigued, we tend to make decisions that are easy and not necessarily aligned with our goals. We lose our willpower, and our self-control becomes impaired. This is the time we are most likely to derail from achieving our goals. Keeping our eye on the prize helps keep us motivated and on track to achieve our goals. Hardwiring habits allows us to make fewer decisions, which limits our mental fatigue and allows us to make better decisions.

CREATING AHA MOMENTS

Oprah coined the phrase "Aha moment" to describe those flashes of understanding that seem to come out of nowhere. Have you ever been in the shower or lying in bed when out of the blue a thought pops into your head that suddenly explains something you have been thinking about? An aha moment is a flash of wisdom that generally comes to us when our minds are in a relaxed and open state of awareness. We all experience those moments when something we have been working hard to figure out suddenly pops into our heads as clear as a bell. All of the blood, sweat, and tears are forgotten, and suddenly, the wisdom comes to us. Aha moments are the best kind of gift we can give ourselves—the kind that feel like you're riding a unicorn through a rainbow with a handful of gift cards and Skittles while drinking a chocolate milkshake.

Daniel Goleman, author of *Focus*, found that we have different varieties of attention that each serve us in a unique way. Our attention level is always somewhere on the spectrum between bored, optimal performance (flow), and frazzled. All of these are helpful to us in the right place and in the right proportion. When they get out of place or out of proportion, they can cause problems. Goleman found that when we are in "flow," our attention and performance are both at peak levels.We are able to work at the top of our skill set and experience minimal stress. We are 100 percent focused and indestructible. Paying full attention is the gateway to getting into flow or in the zone.

Practicing self-awareness skills allows our brain to get into a relaxed state where we can access more information and create our aha moment.

On the opposite end of the spectrum from boredom is frazzled. These moments happen when our stress level goes far beyond feeling challenged and we are at peak attention. Our brain releases stress hormones, and whatever is preoccupying us gets our full attention. Until we can solve the problem, we can't move past it. If we can't move past it, it keeps playing over and over in our heads like a bad record.

A little frazzle is good. It motivates us to recognize problems and search for possibilities. But when we take up permanent residency in frazzle land, our ability to focus deteriorates, our performance decreases, and our stress can start to cause long-term health effects. Goleman says the next time you are in the shower, be in the shower. Don't think about your meeting, or your errands, or the circumference of your waist—and certainly not politics. Think about being in the shower, the water hitting your body. Be present. You might just get an aha moment while you are in there.

YOU HAVE TO MAKE A GOAL TO SCORE

Knowing our strengths and weaknesses allows us to know when risks are smart and when they should be avoided. When we underestimate ourselves, we miss out on taking risks we are capable of turning into successes. If we overestimate our abilities, we might fail, but we'll learn from it and fail better the next time around. You probably have a friend or relative who continually overestimates their abilities. They are the ass at the party who knows everything, has been everywhere, has seen amazing things, and is ready to tell everyone about it. When we don't understand our strengths and weaknesses, we can come across as arrogant, or "big hat, no cattle" as we say in Texas.

Knowing our strengths and weaknesses helps us set challenging *and* realistic goals. My friend Janet is always planning to run a marathon. She doesn't know what it means to start early or take things slow. She procrastinates on starting her training, then jumps right in a few weeks before the event and starts running several miles a day. Then she gets hurt, sick, or just too tired and gives up on the whole marathon dream for a few months. Janet could definitely build up to running a marathon and complete it successfully, but instead, she keeps setting unrealistic goals and failing. It seems like it would be easy to change this, right? But if change were easy, there wouldn't be hundreds of thousands of books on it. Most of us are not really taught a method of setting goals for ourselves. Successful businesses and successful people rely on SMART goal setting as the formula for creating goals that have all of the essential elements for creating what comes next. The more you practice goal setting, the more natural it becomes, until it is a habit you do naturally without any real effort.

SMART goals are:

1. **Specific:** Be specific about what you are going to achieve.
2. **Measurable:** Determine how you will measure your progress.

3. **Aligned:** Align goals with your overall mission.
4. **Realistic:** Set realistic and achievable goals.
5. **Time-Based:** Include a time frame for achieving goals.

STEP 3: WHERE DO I WANT TO BE/WHERE DO WE WANT TO BE?

The third step in the change process involves knowing what goals you want to achieve. This is your ideal future state, your goals, your dreams; it's the outcomes you are striving to achieve. In business, these might be called your projections, goals, outcome measures, or targets. No matter what you call them, they are what you are striving for, and to see them requires you to see things the way you hope they will be in the future.

EXERCISES

Start dreaming big as you think about what you want your future to look like. Answer these questions. Then get started on setting SMART goals for the areas you are ready to start working on.

What do I want my life to look like in one year?

____

What do I want my life to look like in five years?

____

If I could do any kind of work, what would it be?

____

What have I thought about doing over the years, but have never acted on?

____

If I suddenly found out I only had five years to live, would I change any of the above answers?

____

How to get started with setting your SMART goals:

List your "I'm a 10" areas from your lowest to highest score. The areas with the lowest scores are the ones keeping you up at night. They make you want to yell at your kids, kick the dog, and honk at the person taking too long at the stoplight. They are causing you worry and stress. They are holding you back from reaching your full awesomeness. You can be successful in all areas of your life, even if you haven't yet experienced that success.

1. _(lowest score)_______________________________
2. _______________________________________
3. _______________________________________
4. _______________________________________
5. _______________________________________
6. _______________________________________
7. _______________________________________
8. _(highest score) ______________________________

EXERCISE: List your goals

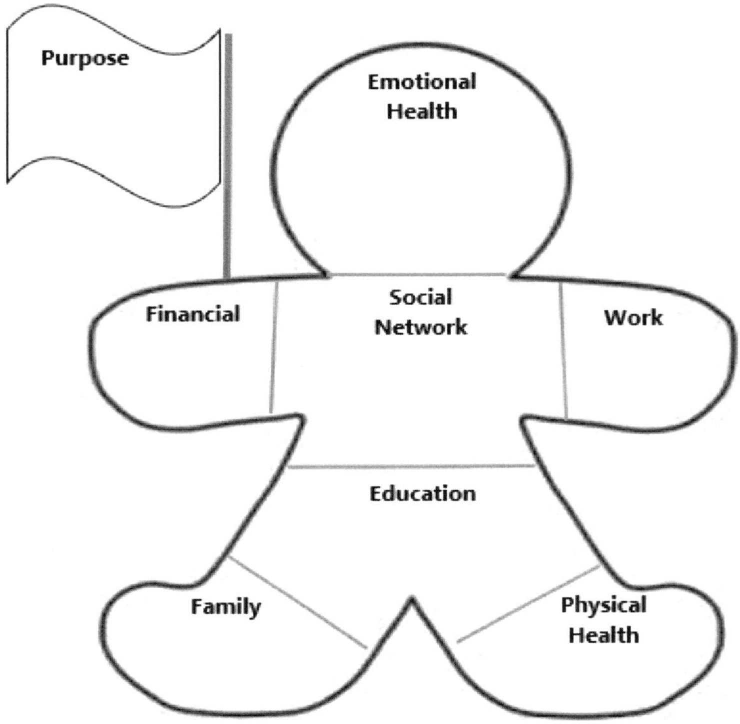

PART III

SELF-MANAGEMENT

CHAPTER NINE

MANAGING YOURSELF WITH CONFIDENCE, COURAGE, AND GRACE

"We are what we repeatedly do. Excellence
then is not an act, but a habit."

— Aristotle

FEAR...THE OTHER F WORD

In *The Art of War*, bestselling author Stephen Pressfield originally intended to write about the writer's block he was experiencing frequently and realized no one was talking about it. He quickly realized it wasn't just writers and artists who experience resistance—it's anyone wanting to move to a higher level. Resistance can occur when you are starting a new gym regimen, dieting to improve your physical health, starting any effort to seek more education, performing new acts of kindness, going from procrastination to having the career you want, etc. Overcoming resistance requires overcoming the fear that you will fail, that you aren't good enough, that you are too busy, too poor, or basically anything else that presents itself as resistance. And that resistance is normal.

On Oprah Winfrey's show *SuperSoul Sunday*, Stephen Pressfield said something that made Oprah stop. I stopped too, and I can only imagine almost everyone watching also stopped and felt a large weight lifted off their shoulders when Pressfield said, "The more important an activity is to your soul's evolution, the more resistance you will have to it."

As I sit here writing this chapter, I think about all the times I have let resistance hijack my goals and dreams, and how a lot of the time I didn't even realize it. I let fear and self-doubt override my goals. We all have stories we tell ourselves that keep our self-doubt front and center as we strive toward a nobler version of ourselves. Our friends and loved ones can add to our stories by bringing their own self-doubt and fear. They most likely don't mean to do it, but as you step out of your comfort zone, it forces them to think about their own comfort zones and what dreams they are leaving on the table in exchange for comfort. Courage is contagious.

Self-management is the ability to effectively manage our emotions, motives, moods, and behavior to overcome all obstacles, real and imaginary, to achieve growth and success. We do not have the ability to determine when we will or won't get swept away with emotion, and in fact, sometimes emotions sneak into our minds and take up permanent residency without us even knowing it.

Self-awareness is the first line of defense in combating self-sabotage and dream killers that we will encounter daily as we fight the battle of feeling scared and inadequate. We don't normally get to decide when an emotion will bring us a smile or tears, cause us to feel jealousy, embarrassment, intimidation, fear, or even smitten, but we do have the ability to choose how we respond.

Managing our emotions does not mean suppressing them, but rather understanding them and using them in appropriate proportion and at appropriate times. We manage them so they don't control us. Managing ourselves can be very challenging since 40 percent of our day is spent repeating habitual behaviors—actions we have repeated so often that they occur naturally and without conscious thought.

GOING PRO

Pressfield talks about the habits of amateurs versus the habits of professionals. As I watched the athletes competing in the recent Olympics in South Korea, I thought about the workouts they had endured, and the time, energy, and money they had spent to master their sports. Lindsey Vonn trained five or six hours a day six times a week and didn't give up when she was injured. Professional athletes compete when they are hurt, practice when they could be doing other things, and push themselves as hard as they can, training their bodies over and over to develop the muscles and habits needed for their sports. During interviews with the Olympians, one of the questions asked over and over was whether they got nervous or scared. None of the athletes expressed fear or anxiety; they all expressed excitement at getting out there and doing what they do.

There is no room for fear or self-doubt when you are in the middle of a McTwist, a chicken salad, a duck foot, or any other snowboarding move. A moment of self-doubt can undo all of the hours of training. These athletes didn't hit the "fear no more" jackpot; they found ways to overcome their fears and obstacles to go after their dreams. I watched them compete in events that sometimes only took seconds; when I listened to their stories, I realized not a single event was exempt from injuries; not a single Olympian was exempt from the loss of loved ones, sickness, hardship, or any other obstacle imaginable. There are always as many opportunities to quit as there are to go on. Self-management skills combined with a clear purpose will keep you focused on what you want and motivated to overcome obstacles that will get in your way.

When I have started feeling like I have done all I can do, I've hit the wall, and I am ready to give up and admit I can't write this book or affect change that will help people achieve their best selves, I think about Katy Perry. We all know her as one of the most successful artists of our time. She is confident, courageous, and successful. But before she became a household name, she was a struggling artist who came close to success a few times, just to have things go badly with the record label at the last minute. She even had three cars repossessed as she continued to move toward achieving her dream. But despite her journey being hard and scary, she says it would have been more uncomfortable not to do it.

Perry has the habits of a professional, not an amateur—that commitment can only come when you are all in. When you're all in, you know it's right, deep inside, and though there may be brief doubts and quick moments when you think about giving it all up, you know if you don't do it, you will be wondering *what if* for the rest of your life.

Here's something else to think about. Excitement and fear both cause the same physical response: the heart rate speeds up, the muscles tighten, and you start to perspire. So what would happen if instead of thinking, *I am scared. I am so scared*, we started thinking, *I am so excited—excited because I am confident I will do my best, I am prepared, and I am courageous*?

SELF-MANAGEMENT SKILLS

Emotional Self-Control: Although we all have probably been tempted to drag our keys down the side of someone's car, carve our names into seats, take our Louisville Slugger to both headlights, and slash all four tires like in Carrie Underwood's song, we realize it's not a good idea.

Sure, we have probably all felt like the actors in *Office Space* when they realize their jobs are completely unfulfilling and boring, and it's time for a change. You take a job intended to pay the bills until you can do what you really want to do, and before you realize it, you have spent years in a job you dread working for a boss you hate.

Do you just walk out? Do you stay because you need a job while you look for something better? Do you try to make it a better place to work? Do you even realize it's a crappy job that's sucking the life out of you? Something is going to happen next, and you get to control how you respond to it, or how you react to it.

Self-management doesn't mean supressing your emotions or trying to sweep them under the rug. It means looking at them rationally before you react irrationally. The heat of passion has led many to utter, "I was so mad I wasn't thinking," "It happened so fast I just reacted without thinking," or "I really put my foot in my mouth this time." We've all had those moments we wish we could take back—wishing later we would have responded rather than reacting.

Responding involves connecting our heart and mind to make responsible decisions we can feel good about—decisions aligned with our purpose, beliefs, and goals. When we repeatedly act irrationally, we create a movement of irrational decision making. This creates our character, and ultimately, the quality of our life. The more you know about who you are and what you stand for, the clearer you can be about your goals and dreams, the people fanning your flame to help you get there, and the people trying to put your flame out. Move toward the flame fanners.

Transparency: Many definitions of transparency exist. Most hinge on transparency as the quality of being easily seen through. Whether talking about people, organizations, or governments, when we talk about being transparent, we are talking about being able to see what we say matches what we do. We are most transparent when we are being our most authentic self. I once tried to impress a guy by leading him to believe I was a more skilled cook than I could ever possibly be. My efforts unravelled, like most other lies, once I had cooked for him the only four things I knew how to make well. My cooking turned out to be far less impressive than I had boasted, and I felt pretty ridiculous.

Trying to be something you aren't is exhausting. Learning from others, taking advice, and mimicking their successful habits are all fantastic ways to improve yourself, but at the end of the day, you are you, and you are the only person in the world who can be you. Being authentic to yourself involves knowing and understanding who you are and what you stand for, being honest with yourself and others, and showing integrity and trustworthiness. Trust and transparency go hand in hand. Trust is the foundation of meaningful relationships.

Adaptability: A great friend and fellow entrepreneur once told me, "If things are going really great now, that will change, and if things aren't going well right now, that will change too." Being able to adapt to change is a great skill to have in any setting. It gives us an advantage in business. Adaptability skills determine how long we are going to dwell on the problem before seeing the possibilities. Our ability to adapt is influenced by the connection we have to what is changing and our mental state at that time. When stress levels are high, adapting to something new is difficult due to the frazzled state of our attention.

Adapting requires us to be flexible to changing situations and circumstances. Our ability to adapt to the environment we live in is what keeps us from becoming extinct. If you desire more than just preventing your extinction, get out there and try new things. Be courageous and confident about adapting to new things.

Remember, before Michael Phelps trained to become an Olympian, he had to find the courage to get in the pool the first time. Before Adam Levine reached superstar status as an actor, TV personality, and the lead singer of Maroon 5, he had to overcome his fears and self-doubts and get on that stage for the first time. Darius Rucker, lead vocalist of the Grammy Award-winning rock band Hootie & the Blowfish, released a solo R&B album in 2002 that did not make the charts. Then Rucker reappeared six years later as a country artist and had several number one hits. In 2009, he became the first black American to win the New Artist Award from the Country Music Association. His recent song, "For the First Time," asks us the important question of when we last did something we haven't done before.

Achievement: An achievement is something accomplished with great skill, effort, and courage. We are motivated to work toward the things important to us. Sometimes the best part of an achievement is what it means to the people who supported us along the way. Each achievement brings us closer to where we are meant to be and builds our self-confidence. Elizabeth Gilbert, author of *Eat, Pray, Love*, once said, "The only boring people I have met are people who are bored." Are you bored, or do you have something exciting and challenging you are looking forward to achieving?

Initiative: Oprah says there is no such thing as luck. There is being prepared and seizing opportunities. Initiative is the power or opportunity to act or take charge before others. When we have a clear understanding of the problem and the possibilities, we can see creative solutions and take initiatives others can't see yet.

Optimism: The word optimism comes from the Latin word, *optimum*, meaning "the best thing." It is seeing the upside in events, feeling hopeful, and being confident about future events. Optimism is the best thing. Optimism gives us hope and positive energy to work toward achieving our goals. It keeps our brains primed to look for other positive things that might help us reach our goals.

Motivation: Our emotions motivate our thoughts, actions, and behaviors. Motivation is the act or process of motivating ourselves and others. The more valuable the opportunity is to us, the more motivated we will be to achieve success.

EXERCISES

Remember, you are the master of your thoughts and actions. Managing yourself involves understanding who you are and where you want to go. Answer the following questions.

I feel like I am being the best version of myself when I am:

____

____

____

____

I feel like the best version of myself when I am spending time with:

____

____

____

____

I feel most motivated by:

____

____

____

____

I am the master of my emotions: (circle answer)

Never	Sometimes	Often	Most of the Time	Always

CHAPTER TEN
GETTING THERE

"The path from dreams to success does exist. May you have the vision to find it, the courage to get on it, and the perseverance to follow it."

— Kalpana Chawla

ARE WE THERE YET?

Kids today cannot fully appreciate the good ole days of traveling long distances in the car with your family and no smart devices. The joy of fighting with your siblings for looking at you, spotting license plates before your dad, playing *I Spy* with your siblings, and of course, asking every five minutes (at least) "Are we there yet?" We never seemed to be there yet! Mom would have a huge paper map spread out all the way across her lap and halfway up the windshield that she couldn't begin to read as quickly as my dad could turn on new streets that she couldn't find either. As kids, we appreciated all of the planning and implementing that goes into creating unforgettable family road trips about as much as we appreciated listening to our parents' music and not having air conditioning in the backseat. In our minds, the time we spent getting to our destination just seemed like the last thing we had to do before really starting our vacation.

It is easy to get wrapped up in this mindset of "When I get there, I will be happy," "When I graduate, I will be happy," "When I land this job, I will be happy," "When I am successful, I will be happy," "When I get a boyfriend, I will be happy." We have all most likely had this mindset, or still do because we were raised with the belief that being successful will make us happy. In recent years, the deaths of Robin Williams, Kate Spade, Michael Jackson, and Prince have shocked us and brought to light the question of what it means to be successful. The shock of such highly successful people being so unhappy has sparked a lot of conversations about what success truly means. Is success just reaching the top of your profession or making a lot of money even if you aren't happy, or is it enjoying the journey and the success along the way? Since we will set and achieve many goals throughout our lifetimes and experience many different levels of success on our journey, it does make sense to enjoy the entire journey of life, and research shows that feeling happy, in fact, helps us to be successful.

It is the journey we call life, and as you may have heard, it's good, it's short, and it can also be a bitch. It is where the action happens, and it will take discipline, motivation, commitment, and an optimistic attitude to get you on the right path to achieving your goals. You will likely encounter many obstacles. Some obstacles will come from the outside world and some will come from within you. They will make you want to stop and turn back to where you were comfortable before. Comfort is like wearing a pair of plush, baggy sweats on the couch on a rainy day while binging on Netflix. It feels good, but it gets boring in a hurry. We aren't naturally wired to be stagnant or stuck in a rut, but that doesn't stop us from ending up there sometime during our journey.

GOING PLACES

Have you ever just stopped, looked around, and thought, *What am I doing here?* One day a few years ago, I was suddenly pulling into my driveway when I realized I didn't remember driving home. It was as if I had gotten into my car and, suddenly, I was already there. I can't explain what happened or even if anything happened at all. All I know is that part of my journey home from work was a big blur.

Life is about going places. We are always going to work, going to eat, going to bed, going to practice, going to the gym. These are the things we do and the places we go day to day to meet our needs, responsibilities, desires, etc. These are the front-line actions and processes we participate in every day. Sometimes we repeat these processes so often they become habits, and before we know it, we are on autopilot, driving home from work. As our self-awareness skills increase, and we start getting a clearer picture of what's important to us, our priorities change.

Our processes will most likely need to change as well to facilitate reaching our new goals and priorities. Henry Ford once said, "If we keep doing what we've always done, we are going to get what we have always got." Our ability to adapt, change, and grow develops our character and our destiny. Our successes and failures and how we respond to them are all part of the journey from where we are to where we want to be. Our thoughts and beliefs continue to guide our actions through every step. Just thinking about how important a goal is can motivate us to do things we would not push our bodies to do otherwise. Would you drive all night and wait in line six hours to see a band you kind of like? Could you train four hours a day, seven days a week to be a competitive tennis player if you didn't really like tennis that much and didn't aspire to win the US Open? Probably not. When something is important to you and you know it deep in your soul, there isn't an obstacle, detour, or roadblock big enough to stop your journey. Getting there is the "how" to your "why." Your why is the thing that keeps you motivated and optimistic to achieve your goals.

LEADING OUR ACTIONS

Trustworthiness, optimism, adaptability, achievement, and motivation are words posted on the walls and websites of just about every organization and school in the United States. These are the core values and characteristics leaders hope their employees and students will have. These are the skills that help us overcome obstacles and challenges to achieve our goals and experience success. They are our self-management skills, and they help us manage ourselves and our actions in getting to where we want to go.

It was obvious Art Schlichter was going to break all kinds of records when he was just a young boy first stepping out onto the football field. I mean, as obvious as a Captain Obvious revelation. He had the magic arm, so there was no doubt he would play in the NFL one day if he could stay physically healthy. And he did. He was the fourth pick in the 1982 NFL draft. However, the only thing Schlichter loved more than football was gambling. His gambling addiction spanned four decades and led to ten-year sentence in federal prison for stealing thousands of dollars to feed his gambling habit. Schlichter was so addicted to gambling that he was even busted for gambling while in prison. He is a permanent fixture on the NFL's Top 10 Draft Busts list. His addiction was bigger than his ability to self-manage his actions.

Michael Jackson captivated audiences of all ages with his unprecedented performances. Generations of fans adored him. Musicians wanted to be him. Dancers wanted to move like him. We all wanted a little bit of the success he had, which makes it hard for us to understand how he could feel like he wasn't good enough. Even after his most impressive performances, he would critique himself and think about how he could have done it better. Jackson was a perfectionist who felt immense pressure to perform at a superhuman level. Millions of people around the world were singing his words, practicing his dance moves, wearing leather jackets in the heat of the summer, and wearing just one glove in the cold of winter. Whatever he did, we did—or tried to do. We wanted just a fraction of his success. And all the while we were looking up to him, he didn't feel like he was good enough.

Schlichter and Jackson were extraordinary men with ordinary problems. Sure, my worrying about being a good enough parent, or your worrying about being a good enough welder, nurse, teacher, leader, etc., and our children's worries about not being cool enough might appear different from Jackson's worries. But, underneath, they are all the same. All worries come from the thoughts and beliefs shaped by our experiences.

When we are young, we can't always manage our experiences. As we get older and are able to manage more of our environment, we learn what it means to manage our time, our money, and the other external components of life. We also learn how to manage the internal components, learning to balance what we have learned and experienced growing up with what we are learning now and what we want to learn in the future. Managing our heads keeps us on the map. If we are on the map, then we are not lost. We may not know exactly where we are, but we're not lost.

Managing ourselves means we need to pay close attention to the stories we tell ourselves. Those stories can be more difficult to manage than any obstacles we can clearly see blocking our paths. "I am not good enough, smart enough, or tall enough." "I have bad hair, I am broke, I am too old, or I am too young." Whatever it is you are telling yourself, remember to be kind with your words and accurate with your thoughts. Don't have conversations with yourself that you wouldn't have with a friend. You wouldn't tell your friends they aren't pretty enough or talented enough, or that they are dumb or fat. We often talk to ourselves much more harshly than we ever talk to anyone else. I think about this when someone is talking really ugly to me. I think about how ugly they must talk to themselves. It brings me some peace knowing I just have to listen to their bull for a few seconds, but they have to listen to it 24/7.

I am very blessed and grateful to be rewriting some of my stories that just don't serve me anymore. Think of the stories you tell yourself. Finding the sweet spot between motivating yourself with stern and tough love and verbally abusing yourself can be a fine line. Be kind to yourself...you are worth it!

PDSA: PLAN, DO, STUDY, ACT

PDSA is a shorthand method for testing change. It resembles the scientific method we learned in grade school science when we tested a hypothesis or experiment. We plan the project, gather our supplies, get all of the instructions, and do the experiment. Then we study the results and act on them. Remember, you are trying out (experimenting with) different paths on your map to get where you want to go. You have to collect information and plan your options, then study the path you choose to make sure it is taking you in the right direction. If you are off course, you make the needed changes and continue the cycle of PDSA until you get on the path that will take you in the direction you want. When you are on the right path, your goals align with your actions, and you might even sense a little tingly feeling in your gut. It feels good to be in alignment.

New activities create new habits that edge out old, worn-out habits, and before you know it, you actually like kale and wear white after Labor Day. You may have done these PDSA cycles at work for quality improvement. In reality, you have probably been doing PDSA since you were a kid, and you are already a pro at it. You just don't know it yet. I have met some homeroom mothers and team moms who are better at managing projects than most professional project managers who have been trained.

Here's how the PDSA process works:

Plan: Develop a plan of actions based on the information you have gathered from Steps 1-3.

Do: Implement the plan. If the project is large, a smaller pilot project can be easier to manage and study.

Study: Analyze the information and study the project's results.

Act: Make changes as needed, and put measures in place to support continued success. Initially, keeping up your new habits will require self-discipline, motivation, and commitment. Putting visual reminders in place during the early stages of transformation will help you stay on track until the habits set in and become more automatic, requiring less effort. You can use this extra effort on something else...anything you want. Think of the possibilities!

Once you apply PDSA, you'll be off and running toward your goals with confidence and courage. List the required actions for achieving your goals. Goals don't get scored without effort. Your actions are the effort you put toward achieving your goals. Setting a goal without an action is like buying the Weight Watchers' manual, never opening it, and expecting to achieve your weight loss goals or buying a stationary exercise bike for your home and then hanging your laundry on it.

STEP 4: HOW DO I GET THERE?

The fourth step in creating successful change is implementing the actions, behaviors, and habits that will get you where you want to be. It is the process of aligning your actions with your thoughts so you can mange yourself in the way you want to. We can't always control what happens to us, but we control how we respond to it.

EXERCISES

Start thinking about the things that cause obstacles, roadblocks, and detours to your success path. Ask yourself these questions:

Which things in my environment will help me reach my goals?

___

___

___

Which things hold me back?

___

___

___

Who fans my flames and supports my success?

___

___

___

Who throws water on them to snuff them out?

___

___

___

What are five things I can do right now to help me achieve my goals?

____

____

____

INSTRUCTIONS FOR EXERCISE

List the actions you are going to take to achieve your goal. Start with one or two areas. Every goal must have at least one action, but it may have as many as needed. Remember the KISS method…Keep It Simple, Sweetie. If you need to sleep in your workout clothes to get to the gym in the morning, avoid the cookie aisle to resist Mint Oreos, or keep all of your facial products on top of the bathroom cabinet so you don't forget to use them, list these actions. Then implement your actions. Start working your plan to see how it is working for you. Study your actions and the results they are bringing you. Make tweaks and adjustments when needed to continue acting on your goals until they are fine-tuned and leading you to your success. These are the actions that lead to your success and the ones you will hardwire as habits of continual growth.

EXAMPLE: SAM WITH GOALS AND ACTIONS

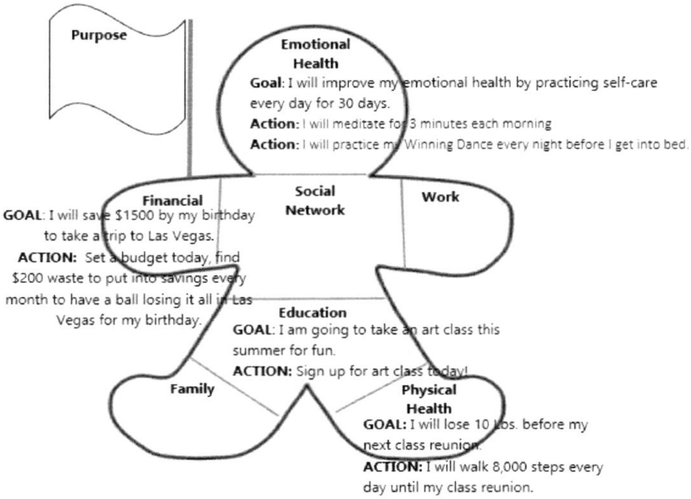

EXERCISE: List your goals and actions

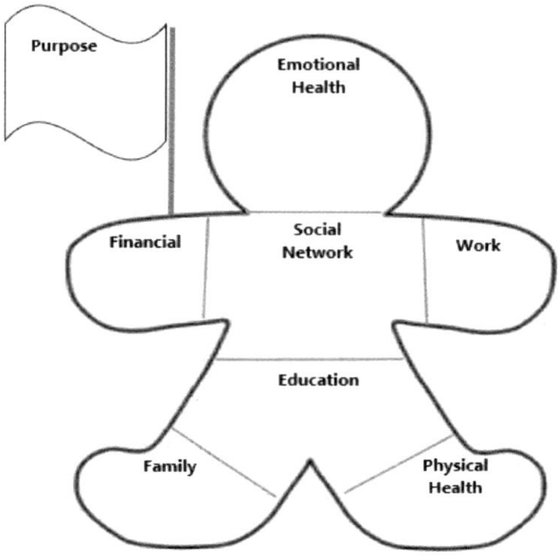

CHAPTER ELEVEN

MAINTAINING SUCCESS

"Habits allow us to go from 'before' to 'after,' to make life easier and better. Habit is notorious—and rightly so—for its ability to direct our actions, even against our own will, but by mindfully shaping our habits, we can harness the power of mindfulness as a sweeping force for serenity, energy, and growth."

— Gretchen Rubin

YOU ARE NOT ALONE

Do you have an exercise machine in your house that functions as a small closet? Do you find vitamins in your cabinet and wonder when you stopped taking them and why? Have you ever hunted through your ashtray to find a cigarette butt after you quit smoking? Do you have a gym membership you have not used in months? You're not alone! In fact, research show that only 8 percent of New Year's resolutions are still going after a year. It takes discipline and self-management to replace less desirable habits with better habits. Discipline is a muscle subject to fatigue, and when it falters, you may find yourself right back where you started. When discipline runs out, we lose our ability to resist distractions and old habits.

Each time we perform a new activity, we are seeing the very beginnings of a habit. Think of the neural pathways in your brain as being like country roads, main streets, and superhighways carrying information to the different parts of the brain. The little country roads are new habits and the superhighways are your old habits that have been repeated over and over to create a large superhighway of information. Repetition creates habits that require less discipline to perform than new habits.

The goal is to practice the habits that work well for you and turn them into superhighways before the discipline muscle wears out. Practice makes perfect, and practice makes habits. Habits require little or no effort to maintain and make life easier.

OH, I CAN'T DECIDE

Have you ever noticed that Mark Zuckerberg, CEO of Facebook, and Steve Jobs, CEO and co-founder of Apple, always wear the same thing? Zuckerberg has a closet full of gray T-shirts and jeans, all alike. Jobs wears a black turtleneck. Both of them explain this as a way to preserve their decision-making abilities for the things that really matter to them. With the massive increase in information that our brains must process each day, decision fatigue is becoming more and more prevalent in our everyday lives. Decision fatigue is the deteriorating quality of decisions made by an individual after a long period of decision making. It has been the subject of many studies and is thought to be the cause of irrational trade-offs in decision making.

Creating the best environment for making the best decisions is important for achieving and maintaining your success. When decision fatigue sets in, we make decisions without putting much thought into them. If we are feeling vulnerable and lonely, we might dial up an ex, even though we swore not to. We may do things like agree to let our kids have an extra hour of screen time so we can have an extra hour of wine time. We might pick up fast food rather than make a sandwich. When we are fatigued, we make decisions more in line with our old than our new habits. They are comfortable at the end of a hard day. Let's face it; comfort feels good when you are in that moment, but not nearly as good as sweet success will feel when you have achieved your goals.

Success feels exhilarating and scary at the same time. It feels alive. Jen Sincero, author of *You're a Badass*, writes with distinct humor and a no-nonsense approach to getting out of your head and on with your life. She gives great advice throughout her book, but one of my favorite bits is when she talks about deciding to quit smoking after several unsuccessful attempts. Sincero decided to adopt the mindset of a non-smoker when she caught herself obsessing about how to be a non-smoker. When she had an urge to smoke, she reminded herself she was a non-smoker. This stopped her from having to make any decisions about what comes next. "I'm a non-smoker," she told herself, and she remained disciplined in telling herself that until the habit of not smoking came naturally and required less and less effort. Decision fatigue can send us running back to our old habits without even realizing it.

STAYING HUNGRY

Shark Tank entrepreneurs Mark Cuban and Daymond John don't agree on most things. However, one thing they do agree on is the importance of hustle when it comes to success. Cuban calls it "staying hungry," and Daymond wrote a book about it titled *The Power of Broke*. They describe it as the mindset of not getting so comfortable that you forget you still have work to do.

Hustle keeps us focused and moving in the right direction. It takes initiative, self-confidence, and courage, and when it is adopted as a mindset, it becomes a habit of continual growth and can maintain long-lasting success. Individuals and groups of individuals who operate with a mindset of continual growth have an advantage over those who don't. While most of us are not and will never be Olympic athletes like Shawn White, Lindsey Vaughn, and Simone Bile, we all have some kind of Olympic-size talent—something we are good at that brings us joy, challenge, and excitement. Something we dedicate our time, energy, and money toward.

Olympians first have to love their sports. Without a deep passion and hunger to win, they could not make themselves endure the grueling workouts year after year or forgo other opportunities like starting a family or taking on a new career. They sacrifice greatly to become Olympic athletes, yet when you hear them talk about their lives and their training, you rarely hear them talk about sacrifices; they talk about the thrill of the challenges, the elation of winning, and the support of loved ones, fellow athletes, coaches, and fans. They train their minds and their bodies and are in the habit of living their lives as professionals and not amateurs.

Whether your Olympic-level skills are in ballet, singing, cup stacking, computer coding, chess, gardening, woodworking, cooking, teaching, piano playing, parenting, friendship, or financial management, people who have a professional mindset are able to maintain their successes over the long run.

SHOW ME WHO YOUR FRIENDS ARE

As a teenager, I couldn't fully appreciate that my parents wanted to meet my friends and their parents, particularly if I wanted to spend the night at a friend's house. Having teenagers myself now, I can fully understand the importance of knowing who your kids are spending time with. "Show me who your friends are and I will show you who you are." As it turns out, Mom was right (again).

Whom you spend time with makes a difference in the quality of your life. It has been said that you are the culmination of the five people you spend the most time with. Are the people you spend your time with fanning your flame, or are they spraying it with the water hose? Your environment and the people in it can determine how successful you are at achieving and maintaining your successes. Setting up your environment for success, surrounding yourself with people who care about you and your success, and creating a physical environment that promotes achieving your goals is important.

Clearing our environment of the things that bring us stress, failure, temptation, or even bad energy keeps us organized and focused on what we want, rather than where we have been. Feng shui is a home-design method based on the ancient Chinese yin yang theory. The balance of yin and yang create positive energy. The balance of calm and active energy in our homes and in our lives creates the positive energy we thrive on. Yin energy includes calm colors, soft music, and water features. It gives off a passive energy that promotes a calm and soothing environment. This passive energy works great in spaces where relaxation is important, like our bedrooms and living rooms. Yang, or active, energy includes vibrant colors and sounds, upward energy, tall plants, and bright lights. Active energy works great in offices, kitchens, and game rooms. Creating a yin yang balance for a feng shui home is thought to be an optimal environment for achieving balance and success.

A LITTLE GRATITUDE GOES A LONG WAY

Every morning when I wake up and step outside (after I make my coffee, of course), I take a moment to be present and thank God for the beautiful sky, the trees, the grass, the fresh air, and everything I am grateful for in that moment. Whether we are giving gratitude or receiving gratitude, it is a good thing. It's a win/win situation. When we give gratitude, we win by raising our positive energy through focusing and appreciating the things that bring us joy. When we receive gratitude…well, it is just plain awesome! It helps us to feel important and valued. Spiritual thought leaders know the power of gratitude in helping us achieve success. It is one of the primary methods used to focus on the positive as opposed to dwelling on the negative, but you don't have to be a spirirtual guru to live your life with gratitide. "Alright, alright, alright," were Matthew McConaughey's first words ever spoken on the big screen back in 1993. *Dazed and Confused* is the movie that introduced us to McConaughey, but it very well could have been his reaction when the director got a wild idea and decided to shoot McConaughey's first scene early. McConaughey describes stepping onto the movie set for the first time ever in his life and feeling excited and nervous. That evening, as he started settling into his trailer, he was feeling good about his first scene that was scheduled to shoot in a few days. All of the sudden, the director was calling for him on the set. McConaughey's heart was racing as he rushed to the set where the director told him they were going to shoot an impromptu scene right then and gave him a very brief description of the scene, including three things about his character. Rather than freaking out and getting all dazed and confused about what to do next or dwelling on the things he didn't know, McConaughey practiced a little gratitude for the three things he did know about the scene and his character. McConaughey often recites affirmations as part of his daily routine. "Alright, alright, alright" was his affirmation of gratitude for the three things he did know about his character. This is an example of how this gorgeous man lives his life with gratitude and the ability to focus on the positive. More than twenty-five years later, we are still saying that one little word repeated three times: Alright, alright, alright!

Achor's study found that the happiest people are those who enjoy the process or the journey as much as the victory. He found that when people didn't enjoy their journey, but instead only wanted to revel in the victory, they were often left feeling unsatisfied and unfulfilled. Think about the people you know or famous people you have read about who have achieved great success and truly enjoy what they do. McConaughey is one of those people who loves what he does; he says he enjoys the experience and process of making a movie, and he doesn't think about what happens to the film after that; whether it goes on to be a big hit, bombs, or never even makes it to the editing room, he doesn't really care because he knows he did his best and he had a great experience doing it. On the other hand, Michael Jackson loved performing and creating, but he was also so focused on creating another number-one hit or earning another Grammy. We thought his performances were incredible, but he never felt like they were good enough. Jackson seemed to spin himself into an anxiety-filled rollercoaster trying to outdo his last great thing. He stopped enjoying the journey. One of my favorite Maya Angelou quotes is, "I wouldn't take nothing for my journey now." She is talking about how difficult it can be to enjoy the journey when you are struggling and feeling uncomfortable, beat down, run over, and hung up wet to dry. But at the end of the journey, when you can look back on all of the obstacles you have overcome, all of the goals you have achieved, and all of the lessons you have learned, it's time to celebrate your success.

STEP 5: HOW DO I STAY THERE?

The fifth and final step in the change process is maintaining your success. This step is about maintaining the new habits you have created and ditching the old ones that weren't working for you anymore. Achieving and maintaining success over the long haul is what sets successful individuals and organizations apart from the others and professional athletes apart from intramural summer league basketball players. They've continued to develop, grow, and maintain their skills year after year. When we can't maintain the success we achieve, but instead continue to fall back to where we started, it can feel like we are running in slow motion or even in reverse. It can be exhausting, expensive, and heart-wrenching. It can also be a great learning experience of how to do it differently next time, and by different, I mean better. Fail, then fail better the next time. Failing at achieving your goals when you have given your best effort isn't a failure. It's a test. A test of commitment, discipline, and motivation. The sooner you can hardwire your new habits, the more likely you will succeed in maintaining your success. Because the stronger the habit, the less we have to rely on our discipline muscle. This frees up our brain to conquer other battles, or maybe just frees up some time to relax and enjoy the present. These are the habits that help us get from good to great. They are the habits of champions. They are the habits that keep us moving toward achieving what we are truly capable of achieving. When first adopting new habits, the old habits and the new habits are going to have a battle. The old habits are going to want to hang on and keep you comfortable. The new habits are going to want to kick the old habits to the curb and get on with achieving what comes next. It's going to be uncomfortable and you will get past it. Remember there is no comfort in growth, and no growth in comfort. During the initial phases of change is when the need for support monitors is the strongest. It doesn't matter if you mark your calendar, put Post-it notes all over your mirror stating your goals in pretty purple marker, make a checklist, use a handy app on your smart device, create a group text with friends, make a bet with a coworker, challenge your spouse, or track your progress on the wall in your bathroom like Ernest Hemingway did to track his weight. Just do it. Remember, out of sight, out of mind. Don't let your goals out of your sight. Find whatever method works for you and do it. You are worth it.

EXERCISES

Start thinking about the different ways you can maintain your success. Ask yourself these questions:

What things in my environment continue to help me maintain my success?

____

____

____

____

What things in my environment support old habits I changed because they weren't getting me where I wanted to go?

____

____

____

____

Who continues to support my happiness and success?

Who is holding me back from experiencing my sweet success?

INSTRUCTIONS FOR EXERCISE

Write your goals and actions on a calendar, Post-it note, your bathroom wall, your friend's bathroom wall, or anywhere you will see it daily. Remember it doesn't matter how fancy or how simple your method of maintaining your success is. Just do it! One of my favorite ways to track my progress is using a calendar to record the actions I *intend* to take each day and then recording the actions I *actually* take. It is a powerful visual reminder that can help track progress and sustain success. It feels good to check something off your list. Try it; you are worth it.

PART IV

SOCIAL AWARENESS

CHAPTER TWELVE

EMPATHIZING WITH AND UNDERSTANDING OTHERS

"I've learned that people will forget what you said, people will forget what you did, but people will never forget how you made them feel."

— Maya Angelou

I FEEL YA

Last week, I was at a high school track and field competition watching my son compete. A young man in a track uniform caught my eye. He was talking to a few of his teammates in the concession area, and he was in a wheelchair. I couldn't wait to see what event he was going to compete in or whether he was going to compete at all. I left the track area to go watch my son in the pole vault area. As we walked back toward the track, my son asked me if I had seen the young man in the wheelchair. About that time, we spotted him at the starting line of the 100-yard dash. There he was in his sporty, red wheelchair, racing against other athletes with two strong legs. Everyone in the stadium was on their feet cheering and yelling. I can't put into words what the electric energy felt like in the stadium that day. I can tell you that students, athletes, parents, and even other coaches stopped what they were doing to watch and cheer. Many of them were mimicking his arm movements as if they were racing in their own imaginary wheelchairs or helping him propel his. This young man didn't win the race, but he won so much more. His act of courage in getting out there, even though some might see him as a little different, made everyone sweating there in that hot South Texas stadium a little more courageous.

This brave young man is a leader! His teammates are probably his biggest fans. They are a close team. I could see them all talking with each other, laughing with each other, cheering each other on, and helping him when needed. These young athletes were more than a team—they were a family, and they were having fun.

The more we learn about our brain and how it works, the more we learn how important our social network is to our quality of life. Researchers have discovered what they call mirror neurons—parts of our social brain that were discovered by accident just this decade when scientists started studying two brains at the same time to determine how they communicate with each other. What they found was that these mirror neurons not only fired when the subject was performing an act, but they also fired when the subject observed someone else perform the action.

Again, the same result was achieved whether performing the action or watching someone else perform the action. This explains why so many of us felt immense happiness for the young man in the wheelchair, mimicking his arm movements as if we were helping to propel his wheelchair. It's even the reason we yawn when we see someone else yawn and smile back at someone who is smiling at us.

Steven Platek, psychology professor at Georgia Gwinnett College, says yawning is contagious in about 60-70 percent of people. He found that people with empathetic understanding were more susceptible to contagious yawning. If only I would have known this before I got married twice! I am sure that neither one of my ex-husbands would have passed a yawn test. Platek goes on to say that those with high levels of empathetic understanding are probably yawning as you read this. Yawns don't have to be witnessed in person to be contagious. Seeing photos, footage, and even reading about yawning will spontaneously cause most people to do the same. I can't tell you how many times I have yawned while writing this…it's a lot.

Our connectedness to others can be complicated. It includes understanding and knowing ourselves so we can understand others and connect with them. Empathy is the primary skill for mastering social awareness. It is the ability to sense others' feelings, needs, and concerns. It is the capacity for understanding what others are saying and feeling and why they feel and act as they do. Being in tune with our own feelings allows us to understand others' feelings and behaviors, which is important for developing and maintaining important relationships with friends, family, coworkers, and teammates.

Daniel Goleman is a pioneer in understanding empathy and how it is connected to success, leadership, meaningful relationships, and performance in every area of our lives. Empathy is the primary skill of social intelligence. Goleman found three kinds of empathy: Emotional Empathy, Cognitive Empathy, and Empathic Concern. Each type has pros and cons and serves a different purpose. Let's look at each one.

Emotional Empathy

Emotional empathy is the kind of empathy we experience when we feel with other people. More than just understanding how they feel, we feel what they are feeling. Emotional empathy is associated with feelings of resonance and a sense of harmony between individuals, among teammates, and even between complete strangers crossing paths for a brief, shared moment. Emotional empathy creates feelings of belonging, inclusion, and safety—all of the things that nurture rapport. Harvard professor Bill George says that business leaders think of empathy skills as soft skills. They consider making their numbers the hard part of their job and understanding, motivating, and communicating with employees the soft or easy part. George says that's backwards. Resonating with others and creating an energy of respect and concern is the hard part. He encourages students in his Harvard business classes to be authentic leaders in life and at work.

Empathic Concern

Empathic concern is the ability to understand how others feel and to communicate through our actions. To walk in someone else's shoes is pointless if you can't process the lesson through your own awareness and experiences. I have a friend who recently had a medical scare. She has been a dietician for years and is really passionate about working with diabetic patients. She has worked with hundreds who have just recently found out they are diabetic. She helps calm their nerves and ease their fears. None of this helped make it any easier when she was diagnosed with diabetes. She freaked out! Fortunately, she only had diabetes for a few days because it ended up being a false diagnosis; however, she says it has made her a better coach for her diabetic patients because she now understands how devastating and confusing it can be when you first get your diagnosis.

Cognitive Empathy

Cognitive empathy helps us understand how others think, but it does not mean we care about them also. Our favorite stores use cognitive empathy to understand how we shop. They arrange their shelves, display their products, create sales, and even send advertisements to our homes based on what they know about us. Cognitive empathy helps them understand what influences us to buy more stuff. This type of empathy is important for communicating effectively with others. It helps us understand others' perspectives and communicate accordingly in ways that make sense to them. People who are only thinking of themselves can use this understanding of others for their own personal gain. Sometimes this is sinister. Other times, it is nothing more than a political candidate campaigning on what voters want to hear. Cognitive empathy in the absence of the other empathies can be hard to maintain over the long run. It can come across as fake, ingenuine, or even manipulative. It's like saying, "I love you," when you don't really mean it, but you know the other person either really needs or wants to hear it. At some point, it is going to be hard to keep saying you love someone if you really don't.

IT'S MY PLEASURE

If you've ever been to Walt Disney World, you know it is a magical experience and a great example of service orientation. The service is impeccable; the characters are dreamy; the food should be illegal it's so good... it's a fairy tale. You may not have noticed the brilliant planning that went into designing and building the park or the ongoing planning and service that takes place to create a magical experience every time you are there.

Most people generally enter a gate and walk to the right when given multiple options. Walt Disney knew this and wanted the area to the right of the gate to be spectacular and inviting. When you enter Walt Disney World and look to your right, you see Cinderella's amazing castle. It is breathtaking. As you walk a little farther, you start to smell something delicious. What is it? Ahh, it's cinnamon rolls baking in the oven, which brings feelings of comfort and joy. They also make you hungry.

Lucky you, there is a cinnamon roll store just around the corner. The cinnamon roll smell isn't actually coming from the bakery. It is delivered through diffusers and piped out to the street where a passerby can get a whiff of that sweet, cinnamon roll goodness and possibly buy one.

Disney World doesn't stop there. It also understands that at the end of the day, after families have been at the park for what seems like days to them, they are tired, they are cranky, and they just want to find their car—but they have no idea where it is. They just want to drive home and fall into bed so they can do it all over again the next day. The parking attendants noticed many exhausted families getting frustrated in the massive parking lot trying to remember which lot and row they parked in. In the excitement of getting to the park, the car's exact location didn't make the memory bank, and now they are stuck in one of the massive lots looking for their car among hundreds of others. All you can think about is how good a hot shower to wash off the sweat, mustard, cinnamon roll icing and blue popsicle will feel.

Walt didn't want you to end your day at the park with a bad experience. It wouldn't be the most magical place on earth if it ended on a sour note. Therefore, the parking attendants now keep a log of the time as each row fills up. At the end of the day, park enthusiasts can tell a parking attendant about what time they arrived and the attendant can look at the log to determine where their cars are likely to be. But they don't stop there. The attendants then drive their visitors to their cars' locations in golf carts. Disney World exceeds our customer service expectations every time by understanding how we think and anticipating what we want and need to have a magical experience.

Service-producing industries account for more than half of our US economy and provide close to 90 million jobs. Companies, particularly service-producing companies, benefit tremendously when employees are service-oriented. By that I mean, employees are engaged with their work and their customers; they have personality traits and a predisposition for being helpful and understanding. When employees are engaged, they help to make customers feel valued and important in the same way that parents help their children feel important and valued by engaging with them. Cognitive empathy training in organizations without providing an environment where the other two kinds of empathy are present often results in employee absenteeism, staff turnover, decreased performance, and disengagment due to burnout. It's hard to give what you don't have so if you are feeling unvalued and misunderstood in your work, it will become more and more difficult to value others and serve their needs. When we are at our best, we perform at our best.

WHO'S WEARING THE PANTS HERE?

Political awareness isn't just about Democrats, Republicans, and government. Politics are about having or hoping to have power and influence over others. They can occur anytime there is more than one person is involved in a group. All organizations, families, teams, groups, and individuals have a system for how they are organized, how decisions get made, and how things really work. In my family, my dad was the ultimate decision maker when we wanted to spend the night at a friend's house or when we wanted twenty bucks for the movies, but when it came to most other things, Mom was the final decision maker. In some of my friend's homes, it was different, just as every organization I have ever worked in has been a little different. Most organizations have leaders with titles reflecting their positions of authority and other leaders who don't have a title of authority, but they are still leaders because they influence the people around them. Understanding the politics of any given situation helps you to understand how you fit into the bigger scheme of things.

Understanding who you are helps you understand others and the politics of your environment. If you are a fan of the TV show *Survivor*, you know how important your alliance can be in helping you stay in the game to have a chance at winning the million-dollar prize. Choose the wrong alliance or fail to understand your position in your alliance and you might get voted off the island and out of the game. Not understanding the politics within your organization, church, quilt club, or soccer team won't get you voted off the island, but it might affect your happiness and future within the group.

Abilities, skills, degrees, certificates, and talents may serve as threshold requirements to get you an interview for your dream job or a position on the soccer team, but it is social skills like understanding others and the relationships that exist within the group that helps groups function as a team.

SEEING POSSIBILITIES WHERE OTHERS SEE LIMITATIONS

Developing others sometimes means you have to look beyond what you might think are limitations. Jamarion Styles just needed one opportunity, and he knew it. He knew it deep inside—just one opportunity. Finding that opportunity was so important to him that he went to the community center every week and sat on the bench, hoping, waiting to be chosen to play basketball. The neighbourhood community center was filled with boys of all ages gathering to play pick-up basketball. In pick-up basketball, you sit on the bench until you are chosen to play. If you don't get chosen, you don't play. Styles never got chosen despite showing up and sitting there week after week. Why was he never chosen? Because the other boys viewed him as having a limitation. You see, as an infant, Styles had lost both of his hands due to an infection.

Neither this perceived limitation nor the other boys' reactions stopped Styles from trying out for his middle school basketball team. When he approached Coach Darian Williams on the first day of school and told him he wanted to be on the team, Williams wasn't sure how it could work, but he told Styles to be at tryouts. Later, Williams told CBS News that Styles told him, "It doesn't matter if I get to play or not. I just want to be on a team. I have never been on a team before." Williams didn't know how it was going to play out, but he knew he wanted to give Styles the opportunity.

In the beginning, Styles didn't get to play at all. Coach Williams said he was the hardest worker on the team and was generally the first one in the gym and the last out. Toward the end of the season, Styles got in the game with six minutes left. When he finally got the ball, the crowd shouted for him to shoot it and he did. Styles caught the basketball with his arms and made a three pointer. He got the ball again and made another three pointer. When he goes to the community center now, Styles gets picked to play every time.

Jamarion Styles, you have style and grace! You didn't give up even when almost everyone else would have. Coach Williams, thank you for facilitating opportunity, for being a life-changing agent for so many young people; you've taught them what it means to see strengths in others' diversity. Just like Jamarion Styles, the more you know and understand your strengths and limitations, the more you can understand others' strengths and limitations.

People like Jamarion Styles, who master self-awareness and social awareness skills, understand themselves and how they fit into the world they live in. They are comfortable in their own skins. They have meaningful relationships and often are part of a bigger group. They feel comfortable being their authentic selves, even if it means disagreeing with others in the group. Once you get a deeper understanding of who you are and what you stand for, you can move toward surrounding yourself with others who share the same values and interests, or different interests if you are looking for that. The quality of our social relationships directly influences the quality of our lives, and our social skills directly affect the quality of our meaningful relationships. Our connections with others are vital for our success, happiness, and overall wellbeing.

SOCIAL AWARENESS SKILLS

Here's a quick summary of the social awareness skills discussed in this chapter that we all need to understand ourselves and the world around us, and, ultimately, to succeed in our endeavors:

Emotional Empathy: The ability to feel what another person is feeling.

Empathic Concern: The ability to understand how others feel and communicate that through our actions.

Cognitive Empathy: The ability to understand how others think; however, this does not mean we care about them also.

Developing Others: Supporting and encouraging *others* to *develop* their knowledge, skills, and behavior to enable them to reach their full potentials.

Service Orientation: The ability and desire to anticipate, recognize, and meet others' needs.

Strength and Diversity: The ability to recognize the strength that diversity brings by understanding and appreciating differences.

Political Awareness: The ability to understand different people's motives and behaviors and use this knowledge to navigate relationships.

SOCIAL AWARENESS SKILLS AND CHANGE

Social awareness skills are as important to creating successful change as chocolate chips are for making chocolate chip cookies. Even if you get all of the other ingredients right, do all of the work, and bake them to the perfect shade of light golden brown, if you don't add chocolate chips…it's still not a chocolate chip cookie. Here's how Social Awareness skills facilitate creating successful change.

STEP 1: Define the Problem/Opportunity (and Who's Going with Me).

Our subconscious mind creates all kinds of stories and beliefs that can sabotage our relationships without us even knowing it. Miscommunication, misunderstanding, fear, jealousy, hope, and love are just a few of the troublemakers that complicate relationships. Like old luggage thrown onto a new carpet, old habits can create blind spots and false beliefs about what really lies beneath them. These troublemakers can sabotage our success before we even get started. Social awareness, together with self-awareness, helps us understand ourselves better so we can understand others better. Service orientation hinges on the ability to anticipate what the customer wants and making every effort to provide it.

STEP 2: Where Am I/Are We Now (and Why)?

Social awareness skills help us understand how we fit into our environment at home, at work, in the community, etc. They help us understand and connect with others so we can collaborate and communicate clearly and develop meaningful relationships. We are social creatures, and whom we surround ourselves with is as important to our quality of life and success as what we put into our bodies. Understanding motives and intentions is important for cultivating deeper relationships based on trust and respect. Pay attention to your "gut sense" or intuition to get a sense of what others are thinking and feeling, despite what they may be saying.

STEP 3: Where Do I/We Want to Be?

Meaningful, loving relationships help propel us to where we want to be. Building relationships that develop and serve the wellbeing of others is what leadership is about. Understanding how we fit into our world and seeing the possibilities in ourselves and others promotes growth and achievement in individuals and groups.

EXERCISES

Start thinking about your social awareness skills. Answer these questions:

Do I feel comfortable when I am in a group?

____

____

____

____

____

____

____

____

Circle the answer that best describes the situation.

I pay attention to how people around me are feeling: (circle answer)

Never	Sometimes	Often	Most of the Time	Always

I can feel what others are feeling: (circle answer)

Never	Sometimes	Often	Most of the Time	Always

When other people yawn, it makes me yawn: (circle answer)

Never	Sometimes	Often	Most of the Time	Always

Exercise instructions: I know it sounds so cliché to ask you to think about walking in someone else's shoes, so I won't ask you to do that. Instead, I'll ask you to pay close attention to the conversations and relationships around you. Step back and observe others in your environment. Can you understand their viewpoints, even if you don't agree with them? Do others in your environment understand your viewpoints, even though they may not agree with them? Does your group all think the same? Observe the politics of your group. How do decisions get made? How does communication happen within the group? Understanding your feelings and emotions will help you to understand others' feelings and emotions. Keep practicing and developing your self-awareness skills in order to continue practicing and developing your social awareness skills. You are worth it!

PART V

RELATIONSHIP MANAGEMENT

CHAPTER THIRTEEN

MANAGING RELATIONSHIPS

"Be a person of substance, a person of action, a person who does what they say. Believe that good or bad, everyone comes into your life, and into a relationship with you, for a reason. Whether it is to have an undying love, or whether it is to further define what you want in a relationship remains to be seen."

— Author Unknown

MANAGING YOUR RELATIONSHIPS

Two weekends out of every year, my mom and her friends would take off for a girls' weekend. There were about fifteen of them, and some of them had been friends since junior high. Sometimes they left town for the weekend, and other times, they would all gather at one of their houses and kick that person's husband out for the weekend—or put him on kitchen duty. Mom would spend two weeks getting ready. She had to find a T-shirt with a funny saying she could wear during the bridge games. She would giggle when she got a naughty one and would model it for us as if she were breaking all the rules and loving it. It was hilarious. They would tell dirty jokes, play bridge, and drink when they were younger. As they got older, they continued to play bridge, but the partying turned to sharing pictures of grandkids, and gathering around a fire to talk, laugh, and, of course, tell dirty jokes. Mom's girls' weekends were so fun that my sister and I even crashed them a few times when we were in high school. Mom couldn't tell a joke to save her life, but her friends were some of the finest joke tellers I have ever heard. The jokes seemed even funnier with them wearing their oversized "Where's the Beef?" "Girls Just Wanna Have Fun," or my favorite, "Kiss my Grits" T-shirts. When they all gathered together, the energy was electric.

My mom was a good friend and she had good friends. Today, my mom is still alive but in Stage 6 of Alzheimer's. She doesn't remember most of her friends, but she is happy and doing well, all things considered. She has taught me so much about friendship and what it means to be a good friend. I am also blessed to have wonderful friends in my life, and I think my mom's example and guidance are a big part of that.

Relationship Management is our ability to work well with others and maintain key relationships. It is the fourth and final domain of Emotional Intelligence. It relies on the other EQ skills and involves knowing and understanding ourselves so we can manage our actions in a way that helps us connect with people and create long-lasting relationships. Our relationships create the team we surround ourselves with. Teamwork, influential leadership, and creating change occur not just at work, but in the home, on the field, in the classroom, and everywhere else in the community. The skills we use to inspire others and manage conflict within our families and circle of friends are the same skills we use at work to inspire others and manage conflict. These skills are generally taught to leaders as part of leadership development once an individual shows an aptitude and interest in getting into management.

But what about the rest of us who don't have a leadership title but still are leading ourselves (the most important organization we will ever work for) and our families. We would benefit from having this education to use in other areas where it is important to communicate with and develop others, manage conflict, be inspirational, be a change catalyst, and develop relationships with others we can collaborate and work with.

TRUST: THE SEED OF A GOOD RELATIONSHIP

Significant relationships directly affect the quality of our lives, and trust is the glue that holds relationships together. If trust is broken, the relationship dynamics change. Trust and confidence in ourselves help us develop the skills we need to make smart decisions about trusting others and having confidence in them, their motives, and their behaviors.

Unfortunately, vulnerability is the precursor to trust. Yep, you have to be vulnerable to the other person to develop trust with that person. Being vulnerable can be tricky because we have all had that person we thought was a friend who turned out not to be one after we shared our secrets. Self-awareness helps us figure out who we are and what's important to us so we can figure out what we like to do and find others who like to do the same things.

When I think of trust and vulnerability, I think about a YouTube clip of a little cat and a big dog on the edge of potential bloodshed, most likely cat blood. The cat is hissing with paw drawn and ready to strike. The dog, whose head is as big as the entire cat, is baring its teeth and we can hear a deep, continuous growl. The cat and dog go back and forth, lightly swatting at each other and growling, when all of the sudden, the dog just relaxes and lets the cat swat it over and over without a reaction. Not a growl. Not one tooth showing. No trace of the partially snarled upper lip. The dog lets itself be vulnerable to the little cat. It takes a few seconds for the cat to stop swatting the dog's nose, but once it realizes the dog trusts it, at least enough not to hurt it, the cat stops and begins licking the dog's face. Today, the two have become really close companions. The owner says the two sleep together, and the cat still grooms the dog frequently. What could have been a bloody brawl, instead turned into an unlikely, furry friendship because of just a little vulnerability.

In her book *Daring Greatly*, Brené Brown says that through her research, she found courage is the gateway to vulnerability. Brown grew up like many of us thinking vulnerability was a weakness, but after thousands of hours of research, she found the exact opposite is true. It takes courage and self-confidence to show up and be seen. Brown says courage, trust, and vulnerability are a package deal.

VALUE YOURSELF, VALUE YOUR RELATIONSHIPS

Will Smith, actor, musician, and father, sent a tweet to his son recently telling him how proud he is of him. In the tweet, Smith states the importance of recognizing that everyone does not deserve to have your time. If you look around and see that the people you are spending your time with are going nowhere and doing nothing when you want to be going places and doing great things, you need to reconsider who you are spending your time with. You have a good chance of sharing the same habits as the people you share your life with. If you look around and feel like you are at the bar in the Star Wars movie, it's time to make some changes.

Jen Sincero, author of *You're A Badass: How to Overcome Self-Doubt and Lead an Awesome Life*, says, "When you figure out what you want to do and who you want to be, start hanging around with people who do those things, start hanging out in the places those people hang." If you really enjoy doing something, find more people who also enjoy it and do more of it. Having trust and confidence in yourself and in others, trying new things, having new experiences, and meeting new people require being vulnerable and courageous.

NOW YOU'RE SPEAKING MY LANGUAGE

Happiness, sadness, disgust, fear, and shock are universally recognized. It doesn't matter where you live, a smile is a good thing and shows you are sharing feelings of happiness while a look of disgust lets everyone know, "Houston, we have a problem." Outside of these five basic, universal emotions, it is easier to communicate and understand each other when we are speaking the same language.

My friends and I learned Pig Latin one summer when we apparently had nothing better to do. It is a made-up language formed from English where you transfer the beginning consonants of each word to the end of the word. For example, peanut butter sandwich would be eanutpey utterbe andwichsay. We would have conversations among ourselves where we giggled and honed our ability to speak this exotic new language. We would speak it in front of our parents when we didn't want them to understand what we were talking about and in front of the cute boys we were trying to impress (trying being the key word here). It was much less sophisticated than the emoji-code language teenagers use now, but for the 1970s, it was cool.

I spent several months and countless hours learning Lean Six Sigma and the Japanese words it uses. Most of the program still uses the same terms as when it was first created and used in Japan. It took me months to learn the language and less than two minutes to realize what an idiot I had been!

I was working for a large healthcare organization in England as the project manager for a massive system redesign project to improve patient access to mental healthcare. For this particular project, my small team was going to be working with the Director of the Program Management Office (PMO). At this facility, the PMO was the only department trained on Lean Six Sigma and their job was to help facilitate change efforts throughout the organization. I realized what an idiot I was when the Director from the PMO began to speak. She used big words I hadn't heard before. I was embarrassed because I was supposed to know this stuff, but I had no idea what she was talking about. I thought it might be that my American English was getting in the way of understanding her British English. What was she talking about? Then I looked around and realized the others didn't know what she was talking about either.

As the PMO director asked for information on the project and the planning work we had done so far, she kept using the word "organogram." We had worked really hard on the project and in preparing for the meeting. We were really proud of our work, but she didn't seem impressed with any of it. She looked down her nose and over her glasses at us as she used big words we didn't know. She never offered to explain things to us in a way we understood, even though she must have recognized that we were not speaking her language. The meeting felt more like an interrogation than a project meeting. All that was missing was the bright light shining in my eyes. My team didn't feel very comfortable in the meeting and contributed very little. When the meeting ended and she left the room, we concurred that we had no idea what an organogram was, but we thought we would each like at least two or three of them.

It turns out, an organogram is another (far less used) term for an organizational chart. An organizational chart! You know, like a family tree that shows the relationship of everyone in a particular family. An organizational chart is the same thing for an organization. My point is it doesn't feel good to be excluded, and the way we communicate can intentionally or unintentionally exclude others.

Whether it is with other departments or coworkers, family members, classmates, roommates, neighbors, fast food workers, baristas, or friends, maintaining relationships involves sharing information through all forms of communication. Inclusion is the opportunity to learn different ideas, see others' points of view, build relationships, and create new possibilities.

THERE IS NO I IN TEAM

Ahh…the 1970s. Disco, bell bottoms, the Sony Walkman, VCRs, the first facelift, and the first email. The 1970s are known as a time of pivotal change. The end of the postwar economic boom and the beginning of what author Tom Wolfe coined as the "Me decade." During this time, workers had about 75 percent of the information they needed to do their jobs. Today, research indicates that workers know only about 25 percent of what they need to know about their jobs. The other 75 percent of the information has to come from others involved in the work process. So, communication and team work are more important than ever in the workplace.

Email and fax machines changed the way we communicate and how often we could communicate. Emojis have become a fun part of our communication experience, but they actually solve a problem. When communication is written, we don't get the rest of the message, which is dependent on nonverbal cues. Without the smiley face, thumbs up, or maybe the smiley face with jazz hands, "okay" is just "okay." If your friend texts to ask you to go to a party and you just text "okay," that would have been okay before emojis, but now that you can add some jazz hands to show your excitement about the invite, the fact that you did not can be taken as you're going because you have nothing else better to do. Emojis help convey the emotions and nonverbal communications you would see if you were communicating face to face.

Significant decreases in face-to-face communication are thought to be part of why empathy and communication skills are at all-time lows. Understanding ourselves and others promotes inclusion and new possibilities. Without inclusion, there will always be a "we" and a "they"—there will always be the other, those included and those who aren't. It doesn't matter if you're eight or eighty, it doesn't feel good to be excluded from something you want to be part of.

RELATIONSHIP MANAGEMENT SKILLS

Managing our relationships in our personal and professional lives is essential for our success. We are all leaders of ourselves and the people around us, even if we don't have the title or the income that goes along with it. Managing relationships relies on all four Emotional Intelligence domains. Here are the skills to master so you can manage the relationships in your life:

Influence: The capacity to influence the character, development, or behavior of someone or something.

Communication: The successful conveying or sharing of ideas and feelings.

Conflict Management: Resolving disagreements with grace.

Inspirational Leadership: Guiding and motivating with passion and purpose.

Change Catalyst: Initiating, managing, and leading in a new direction.

Teamwork and Collaboration: Cooperation and team building.

RELATIONSHIP MANAGEMENT SKILLS & CHANGE

Step 4: How Do I Get There?

Our ability to work well and collaborate with others is important for achieving success. The better we are at managing our relationships, the more valuable we are to the group and the overall process. Having relationships that support our goals and dreams is important for our wellbeing and success. Leaders who can inspire others can create an environment where team members are working together toward the same goals.

Step 5: How Do I Stay There?

Surrounding ourselves with people who support our goals helps us maintain our success. Friends, family, coaches, and others can keep us accountable to our actions and grounded in our success. Collaboration with others brings new ideas and information that can add to continued success.

EXERCISES

Start thinking about how you manage the relationships in your life. Circle the answer that fits you best:

I work well with others:

Never	Sometimes	Often	Most of the Time	Always

I get asked to be a part of a team:

Never	Sometimes	Often	Most of the Time	Always

During situations of conflict I often make things:

Better	Worse

Exercise instructions: Continue practicing and developing your self-awareness, self-management, and social awareness skills to help you develop the skills required for managing your relationships. Identify the key relationships in your life and your role in helping the group reach its success. Are you promoting team work and collaboration, or are you hindering it? Who are the people you are influencing? Are you leading yourself and others in developing life skills that will help them achieve success along with you? High-performing groups consisting of high-performing individuals can achieve astounding success. Be that change catalyst to inspires others to be their best and achieve their possibilities. You are worth it!

PART VI

INNOVATIVE FUNDAMENTALS APPROACH

CHAPTER FOURTEEN

BUILDING A THRIVING ORGANIZATIONAL CULTURE

"Customers will never love a company until
the employees love it first."

— Simon Sinek

LEADER…IT'S MORE THAN A TITLE

I learned about leadership long before I knew what I was learning. My parents were self-employed, and I watched them run their businesses and lead their employees until they closed their last store when I was in high school. My sister and I spent many hours with our parents in the stores and even more hours talking about the stores. Mom would chauffeur my sister and me around to all of our activities, and then we would head back to the store to wait on Dad to close for the day so we could go eat. My sister and I would raid the candy machine in the customer waiting area, play hide-and-go-seek, climb inside the huge stacks of tires back in the warehouse, sit on the motorcycles and pretend we were racing each other, and talk with Marcie, Joann, Slim, Gary, and the other people who worked for my parents.

Looking back now, I am pretty sure all of the guys in the shop probably cringed when they saw us coming, except for Slim; he liked us, and we loved him. He would tell us a joke or a funny story every time we saw him—most of them were appropriate. He would ask us about our day, tease us about having boyfriends, and share stories about his kids and grandkids. He was like a grandpa to us. Slim and the majority of the other employees worked for my dad until he closed his last store. I am sure every day wasn't fantastic and all that, but everyone seemed to be really happy there. They worked hard, laughed hard, played jokes on each other, and when it came to one of them needing something, they all had each other's back.

My sister and I didn't realize we were getting leadership training. We thought it was just hanging out with our parents at work so we didn't burn the house down before they got home followed by boring dinner conversations about work. But it was more than that. It was authentic leadership. I didn't understand the terminology they used or the graphs and projections they were looking at, but I understood that it felt good to be in my dad's stores. I understood that my parents cared about their employees—not just their work performance, but really cared about them as people. I understood that Slim, Marcie, Gary, and the crew laughed and joked with each other and cried with each other during hard times. I understood how much my parents meant to their employees when Dad was diagnosed with brain cancer and they brought food, and stayed to talk, laugh, and cry. They didn't come once, but several times, and they kept coming long after the funeral.

It has been thirty years since my dad passed. Now I understand…I understand when I am back in Amarillo and run into someone who worked for Dad. People still remember me after all these years and stop to hug my neck and share a memory of my father. I understand that authentic leaders can have a lifelong influence on the people they lead.

Bad leaders can also significantly impact the lives of the people they "lead." Not in the same way as authentic leaders, but equally as significantly. I have worked under several leaders in my thirty-year work history. A handful of them have been authentic and phenomenal, the kind of leaders you want to show up and give your all for. They were the leaders who inspired everyone to be their best. They were the kind of leaders who didn't have to spend money on programs to teach employees how to be nice to their customers because they showed them every day through their actions. What kind of leader are you?

THRIVING PEOPLE CREATE THRIVING ORGANIZATIONS

Do you remember the first time you ever saw one of your teachers outside of school? When I was in first grade, I saw my teacher, Mrs. Bradley, at the grocery store and realized teachers go to the grocery store and did real people stuff. It seems crazy to think such a thing, but it also seems just as crazy to think people can thrive at work when they are not thriving in life. Can nurses help patients thrive when they don't know how to thrive themselves? Can parents raise thriving children if they don't have thriving habits at home? Can teachers teach students how to thrive if they are not thriving themselves?

Nellie's Free-Range Eggs is an egg company that promises always to deliver certified humane, wholesome, free-range eggs at a reasonable price. Nellie's recognizes that a happier chicken produces a better quality egg. The company's ad campaign says things like, "We love our hens; you'll love our eggs," "A kinder kind of egg," and "Where both the chicken and the egg come first."

Nellie's is the brainchild of Jesse Laflamme, the company's chief executive farmer. He says when he was growing up on his family's egg farm, he had a chicken named Nellie. She was more than an egg-producing employee. Nellie was more like a pet or a friend. When Jesse played in the yard, Nellie was sure to be close by and even rode in the basket of his bike. As a business owner, Jesse wanted all of his chickens to experience a nice work environment like the original Nellie. He wanted a place where employees could balance their work roles with physical exercise, a good diet, plenty of rest, and some time to gather around to scratch and cluck with each other while on break. Imagine if all organizations felt this way about their employees. Imagine if you worked for an organization like this. Imagine if you got to lead an organization like this with happy, healthy employees and happy, loyal customers.

We know people (and Nellie's chickens) perform better under optimal conditions. It might look a little different from one area to the next, but at the core of every employee's needs, wants, and desires are the same things at the core of every human being's needs, wants, and desires—to be seen, heard, and understood. These are basic human desires, and when present, they can cultivate a culture where empathy, respect, and compassion can flourish.

Can an organization elevate itself to the next level if the people who work within it don't elevate themselves to the next level? If employees don't grow with the organization, will there eventually be a breaking point where employees can't perform at higher levels despite the organization's need for more performance? Is that time already here?

WHY CHOOSE "OR" WHEN YOU CAN CHOOSE "AND"?

Imagine if your boss or some project manager hired by your company who has only spent two hours in your department told you: "Somewhere, someone is changing something that will change the way you do your work. We want you to forget about the last process we asked you to embrace without having first requested your input and replace it with a bigger and better process about which you also had no input. It will make your job harder, but it's what we think we need. We'll let you know when it is time to disown this new process and embrace the next new process we create for you, again without your input. Thank you for all of your hard work." These, of course, weren't the words I used as I stood in front of numerous employees to talk about changes in their work area, but it is what a lot of them heard me say and also what they experienced.

Organizations need to be able to change efficiently and effectively to stay ahead of their competition and maintain their viability. This also means employees need to be able to change efficiently and effectively. This can be especially difficult and frustrating since the vast majority of people never get the opportunity to formally (or informally) learn how to create change. Not understanding how to create change, especially when there is more change occurring at a faster pace than ever before, can leave employees feeling like they are hanging onto the end of a rope that is being swung around in many different directions. Research shows that even the most successful organizations fail in their change efforts 50 to 80 percent of the time, which is neither efficient or effective.

I have led nor been a part of many change projects throughout my professional career, including one-on-one instruction with patients at their bedsides to create new, healthier habits and adapt to new physical changes; leading staff and departments in creating better ways of working and adapting to new regulations and standards; and even facilitating massive system redesign projects with multi-million-dollar budgets. Every one of these change projects involved people and processes.

When the people and the processes were both performing at their best, outcomes were consistently good. Even when the process was bad, engaged employees could catch the errors and fix them. However, when the people weren't engaged with their work and performing at their best, it didn't matter how awesome, perfect, or phenomenal the process was; it was still going to fail. Every process that involves people is only going to be as good as any one person involved.

So how do organizations help their employees to be at their best so the organization can perform at its best?

This isn't a new question, but it is a more complicated question now than it was fifty years ago. Employees want more than a discount at the local gym and a chance to be in a weight-loss challenge with their co-workers; they want to be valued and included. When employees can be included in the changes going on in the work area, they can feel included. When employees develop the skills to create successful change, they are learning Emotional Intelligence skills along with Change Management skills so they can improve their own wellbeing and create the changes they want to see in their lives to reach their goals. People create the culture of any organization, and when they are in the habit of continual growth, the organization is in the habit of continual growth. It's a lot like the old adage of, "Give someone a fish and they eat for the day; teach them to fish and they can eat for a lifetime." Teaching an employee to deal with the changes in their work area will only teach the employee how to deal with the new changes, but teach an employee how to create successful change and they can create possibilities throughout their lifetime (which happens to include work).

So I ask you...why choose *or* when you can choose *and* when it comes to employee development, empathy training, process improvement training, project management training, change management training, decreasing employee healthcare-related costs, decreasing absenteeism, increasing performance and productivity, decreasing employee turnover and related costs, and developing effective employee health and wellbeing life skills training and education?

BENEFITTING FROM PERSONAL GROWTH IN A PROFESSIONAL SETTING

As I mentioned in Chapter 6, Simon Sinek, author of *Start with Why*, speaks to individuals and organizations around the world about the importance of starting with *why*. Sinek's mission is for the vast majority of people to feel safe at work, fulfilled by the work they do, and wake up inspired to go to work. It sounds pretty simple, right? It might sound simple, but according to research conducted by Gallup, it is definitely not common practice.

In the United States, job pressure is top on the list of what's stressing us. Citing coworker tension, bosses, and work overload as the primary contributing factors, 77 percent of US workers say they regularly experience physical symptoms caused by stress and 73 percent experience psychological symptoms. If we look at what's going on in the bigger picture of Americans' general health and wellbeing, we aren't doing as well at taking caring of ourselves as we are at contributing to the GDP. This means more of us are showing up to work with depression, addictions, and other issues that keep us from being the best versions of ourselves.

We can't carve our employees out of the bigger picture and ignore the fact that when the population overall has more people suffering and struggling, then the workforce will have more suffering and struggling. It is highly likely our employees, family members, neighbors, kids, letter carrier, and even our UPS driver is struggling along with us. We may never know what people are really going through, but we do know from research collected by Gallup in its massive, ongoing study of employees that no matter where you live or where you work, all around the world and across all industries, if we are thriving, we are twice as likely to be engaged in our work than if we are struggling, and six times more likely to be engaged than those suffering. Thriving employees also have 62 percent lower healthcare costs than those suffering. Gallup research shows 70 percent of employees are not engaged with the work they do. Seventy percent! Can you imagine if only 30 percent of a basketball team showed up to play? Even if the basketball team had LeBron James "The King" on it, it wouldn't win many games. The 30 percent who show up and work hard will eventually get tired of the mediocre performance. They will leave to find other high-performing teammates, and the organizations that can't engage their employees will live in a state of mediocracy.

WHO MADE THAT DECISION?

Ethical decision making is not new. It has been around as long as humans. It is based in the roots of fairness, responsibility, trust, respect, and caring for an individual. In our simplest days, these spoken and unspoken rules kept order in the village and helped decide who would eat first, who got the best loincloth, and who got the safest sleeping place on the soft rock next to the fire. Modern-day ethical decisions are far more complicated—more complicated for individuals and certainly more complicated for businesses. The ability to make an ethical decision is directly related to our level of Emotional Intelligence skills. The organizations that promote these skills raise the quality of ethical decision making within their organizations.

Ethics are based on our internal currency, like our values and morals. However, we frequently measure success using external currency like productivity quotas, sales targets, and hours worked. Leaders and employees face numerous ethical decisions every day. Delivering what shareholders want, customers desire, and employees need can be like pulling a rabbit out of a magic hat while riding on a purple unicorn. Most people don't go into work on Monday and decide they want to start embezzling money from the company or create fake bank accounts to reach their sales targets. People generally start off on the right moral path. Over time, though, pressure to perform can make people waver in their beliefs and actions. There is pressure to keep a job, get a bonus, make a quota, be part of the group, or even maybe just pay the rent. Circumstances, situations, poor planning, and even naivety can put us in situations that challenge our morals and values. It is our self-awareness that keeps us tuned in to whom we are and what we stand for. When we know something is right or wrong, we can confidently stand up for it or against it.

THE POWER OF INCLUSION

In 1788, a small group of Austrian army scouts set out on horseback to check the area around the town of Karánsebes within the Austro-Hungarian territory for any armed Turks they feared would invade the area. It was just before the Battle of Karánsebes, and Austria and Turkey were about to clash. While the rest of the Austrian soldiers set up camp for the night, the scouts left on their horses. The scouts came across a band of gypsies who had a lot of schnapps. The scouts bought the schnapps and proceeded to drink it as if it were going out of style. Pretty soon, the scouts were drunk and belligerent, so much so that when a small group of soldiers from their army infantry showed up and wanted to drink with them, they refused to share. The scouts even went as far as building a makeshift fort to keep the infantry from joining their group. Things got out of hand in a hurry, and someone got excited and fired a shot. The scouts and infantry started shooting at each other.

In all the excitement, the infantry began to shout that the Turks were attacking them. The Austrian scouts and infantry soldiers both thought the Turks were attacking them and continued to shoot at each other, killing many. To make things even worse, the Austrian army was made up of soldiers from several different countries who spoke different languages. So when the German-speaking officers shouted "Halt! Halt!"

the non-German speaking soldiers thought they were yelling "Allah! Allah!"

Many of the soldiers made it back to the camp. With both the scouts and the infantry still believing they had been attacked by the Turks, an artillery strike was ordered by one of the officers. That night an enormous battle ensued, and when the Turks actually did arrive two days later, they found almost 10,000 Austrian soldiers dead and wounded. As a result, the Turks were quickly able to capture the town and the surrounding area.

The Austrian army failed to include everyone in the communication process because they used language that was not understood by all of them. The language we use to communicate is a powerful tool for including or excluding others. Inclusion is the act of being included in something bigger than yourself, and it is a basic human need. It feels good to be included and bad to be excluded. Being included makes us feel like we matter, like we are important, understood, and relevant. It's a basic human desire to want to feel important enough to be included. Employees are no different. They like to be included, too. My dad always taught me to think of employees as customers of the organization. He often reminded my sister and me that it is the employees who show up every day who put the roof over our head and the designer bag on our arms. He called employees the internal customers of any organization. They are customers of the organization because they can choose to work somewhere else. Employees have many different reasons for choosing a job, but when you have good employees, you want to keep them. You could hire a big, fancy consulting firm to come to your organization and evaluate things, or you could just remember that people are people, and they will always be people. People like to be seen, heard, and understood.

I have worked in organizations that practically stopped everything to figure out why a high-performing employee was leaving the organization. I have also worked for organizations that didn't even realize they had high-performing employees working for them and certainly didn't realize when they had left. The second ones are the ones that didn't see their employees as customers. They definitely saw them as expenses later, though, because employee turnover always increases costs since training new employees is expensive.

While writing this book, I chose to leave my leadership positions and work in direct patient care like I did when I first graduated with my nursing degree. It is basically the equivalent of going back to an entry level position. I made far less money, but needed to have less responsibility, fewer hours, and a more flexible schedule to finish my book. If you are at the top of your profession and haven't visited the entry level positions where your kids or grandkids could be entering the workforce, it's an interesting learning experience.

It was a kinder and gentler time when I was entering the workforce. Today, young adults entering the workforce have been dealing with school shootings, seeing wars on TV, and mass shootings at concerts for most of their lives. These young adults are said to have fewer social intelligence skills than previous generations and more of them suffer from depression and anxiety. While it may not be my fault, your fault, or your company's fault, we can all take responsibility by learning how to create the change we want to see. Every person can make a difference in the workplace. Working in an environment that sucks the life out of you is doing a disservice to you. The people around us suffer when we suffer and they thrive when we thrive. We can't accept this situation; we have to be vigilant to do all we can to change it. If you can't make your workplace better, find a better workplace. I believe that as organizations become more knowledgeable about what really inspires and motivates employees to show up and engage with their work, employees will have more chances to choose meaningful and fulfilling work.

I want to believe that now that we know how connected emotional intelligence and change management skills are to success in the workplace and in life, more schools and companies will provide training on them. Imagine how different it could be if everyone had the opportunity to learn the skills for creating change and could be included in more positive change efforts. What if leaders didn't have to guess what would increase performance and productivity, but instead, they trusted their staff had the skills and the desire to make improvements in their work areas? I have worked with employees who repeated bad processes over and over again without even questioning or realizing how ridiculous they were, turning a two-step process into as many as ten steps.

I worry about our children and grandchildren working in some of the environments I have worked in, have heard about, and especially, the ones that have made national news. I work in healthcare where the focus is on healing people, but I have worked for leaders who gladly stepped over people to produce profits. Some stepped over employees to achieve their performance goals. Some stepped over employees and customers to achieve their profits. I believe if we are not part of the solution, we are part of the problem. I also believe we can come together to create work environments where people, processes, and profits all thrive.

EXERCISES

Answer these questions:

What kind of organization do I work for?

____

____

____

Do I look forward to going to work, or do I dread it?

____

____

____

Do I like the people I work with?

____

____

____

Would I want my kids or grandkids to work at an entry level position at my organization?

____

____

____

What are the five things I like most about my job?

____

____

____

What do I dislike about my job?

Do I feel important or valued at work?

Do you feel fulfilled by the work you do?

CHAPTER FIFTEEN

CREATING SCHOOLS WHERE STUDENTS AND STAFF THRIVE

"Those who know, do. Those who understand, teach."

— Aristotle

POSSIBILITIES IN THE CLASSROOM

When my sister and I graduated from elementary school as proud sixth graders, we were excited, but not as excited as we had been a few weeks earlier. In fact, we were mad. My sister and I were mad at our parents, mad at the school system, and basically just mad at everyone because we were pre-teens and that's how we rolled. We were mad because we had just found out that the school boundary lines were changing, so we would be going to a different school than our best friends. Since we were in kindergarten, the school boundaries had been the same, so we just assumed we would be donning the baby blue colors in middle school. My best friend Lisa and I had been inseparable since the first grade and only lived three blocks apart. She lived one block from the new boundary and I lived two blocks on the other side of it. I wasn't going to look good in Kelly green and I didn't want to wear Kelly green. Neither my sister nor I could believe our parents would not sell our home so we could move back into the other school zone to wear baby blue. We were sure we had the meanest parents in the world. We begged and pleaded all summer in hopes they would come to their senses, but that fall, when the school year started, my sister and I showed up to middle school wearing Kelly green.

Of course, our parents were right. I am so thankful they didn't give in to our shenanigans because I would have missed out on meeting Coach Hollabaugh and Mrs. Carter. I feel like my future would have been different if I hadn't been blessed to have these two positive influences in my life. They changed the way I thought of myself as a person, a student, and a leader. Coach Hollabaugh, affectionately called Coach Holly, was my middle school coach. She coached volleyball, basketball, and track, and she was awesome. Mrs. Carter was my cheerleading sponsor and math teacher. They are the kind of teachers you pray your children, grandchildren, and everyone's kids get. They went above and beyond to reach their students and develop them not just as students, athletes, or cheerleaders, but as people.

Today, thought leader Brené Brown is doing some amazing work to bring courage to the classroom. She is a pioneer in areas like courage, shame, vulnerability, and empathy. Brown, who has been interviewing people for more than fifteen years, has discovered that out of the 200,000-plus people interviewed, 90 percent could remember a specific teacher, coach, or administrator who believed in them when they felt like no one else did. She also found that 88 percent could recall a specific incident where they were shamed by a teacher, which changed the way they forever thought of themselves as learners. Brown's in-depth research helps us understand how important our words are to those we are teaching and how learning itself requires a certain level of vulnerability and trust.

My friend Lisa and I recall how more relaxed schools were when we were young. We used to leave school and walk across the soccer fields to her house for lunch without signing out in the office or anything. We would just leave and come back, and we weren't breaking any rules. Back then, a Sasquatch could have picked us up from school and no one would have noticed. We used to walk around the neighborhood without any worries about being abducted or harmed, and the only drills we had at school were for tornadoes and fires. We felt safe. We didn't see war on TV, and we certainly didn't see it in our hallways and cafeterias. Today, my son says he doesn't really think about school shootings much because he doesn't think one will ever happen at his school. I bet each of the 187,000 students attending the 193 primary and secondary schools that have experienced a shooting on campus during school hours since the Columbine shooting in 1999 thought the same thing. As if middle school and high school aren't challenging enough on their own!

UNDERSTANDING OURSELVES AND OTHERS

When my parents were called to the principal's office to discuss an incident in my kindergarten class, let's just say they were less than thrilled. I hadn't even been in school a week yet and I was already in the principal's office. When my parents arrived, I had to explain that I had punched Tommy in the mouth for calling me Toy Truck. My mom had a look of shock mixed with embarrassment on her face as she said my full name—Toie Ann Steward. That's when you know you're in trouble. My dad didn't look embarrassed at all. In fact, he looked a little proud that I had stood up for myself. They, of course, made Tommy and I apologize to each other, and we actually became pretty good playground friends. He never again called me Toy Truck, or Toy Box, Toyota, Boy Toy, Toy Store, or any of the other "funny" names people have creatively invented over the years. He just called me Toie.

Tommy and I were both lacking in social skills, which is pretty normal stuff for kindergarteners. If only all the problems going on in our schools today were that simple. Childhood and adolescence are tough enough with trying to figure out who you are, plus dealing with what your parents want and your teachers and coaches expect. A culture founded on social and emotional intelligence creates an environment where students, teachers, administrators, kitchen staff, and environmental services are all tuned into themselves and others around them. Compassion, understanding, and respect for ourselves and others is all around us when we have the skills to see it. Social and emotional intelligence help us understand what is important so when peer pressure presents itself, we can make good decisions based on who we really are and what we value. Our social and emotional skills are important in every part of life, and they can start being learned when we are very young.

An explosion of interest now exists in adding Social and Emotional Learning (SEL) to the school curriculum to teach the life skills students will need. It is said that IQ will get you into school, and EQ will get you through school. Schools, families, organizations, and communities are increasingly recognizing the importance of promoting the social and emotional competence of youth to facilitate academic, career, and life success.

The Collaborative for Academic, Social, and Emotional Learning (CASEL) is comprised of leading authorities in social and emotional wellbeing and education. CASEL is a worldwide leader in advancing SEL science, evidence-based practice, and policy. It believes that effective SEL programming begins in preschool and continues through high school. It envisions a time when every school in the nation will provide evidence-based SEL programming to all students at all levels.

CASEL has identified five interrelated skills or competencies important for all SEL programming.

- Self-awareness
- Self-management
- Social awareness
- Relationship skills
- Responsible decision-making

SEL programming that carries over into families, the community, careers, and college readiness earns the highest level of CASEL program ranking. Programming that includes mindfulness is also seen as very important in the SEL environment. Imagine being an organization about to hire a new graduate who has already had twelve years of formal education in social and emotional learning, process improvement, project management, and change management. How excited would you be? An employee who has been learning and practicing these skills for twelve years—the skills important for organizations to thrive. Imagine if over the twelve years of learning and practicing these skills, these students involved their families with their homework assignments so the whole family was learning, practicing, and creating habits to promote emotional wellbeing and continual growth throughout the community. Imagine if organizations in the community also focused on promoting emotional wellbeing and continual growth. Think of the possibilities.

WHAT CAN A SEL PROGRAM ACHIEVE IN YOUR SCHOOL?

SEL programs are one of the most successful interventions to promote the positive development of students. Research findings from hundreds of controlled studies indicate that SEL programming improves students' academic achievement and positive social behavior, while reducing their conduct problems and emotional distress.

Longitudinal studies have shown the same results in students as in people lucky enough to work in environments focused on employee wellbeing and growth. Increased social and emotional competence is related to reductions in a variety of problem behaviors, including aggression, delinquency, substance use, and dropping out.

Depending on the nature of the approach, SEL programs can lead to three types of program outcomes: 1) promoting knowledge or skills related to the five competency clusters, 2) creating positive learning environments that are safe, caring, engaging, and participatory, and 3) improving student attitudes and beliefs about self, others, and school. Changes in these individual and contextual factors promote positive social behaviors and peer relationships, reductions in conduct problems, reductions in emotional distress, and improvements in academic performance.

As schools are under increasingly growing pressure to score high on standardized tests, students are experiencing higher levels of anxiety, stress, and depression than any generation before. This is not a workable combination. Stress, anxiety, and depression are at the top of the list for impeding performance. Developing self-awareness skills throughout a school can help teachers, students, and all staff manage their negative emotions like fear, anxiety, anger, depression, and jealousy. Replacing them with courage, self-confidence, and accurate self-assessment will help schools create an environment where respect, empathy, collaboration, team work, and leadership can thrive. It's not my fault, your fault, the teachers' fault, the students' fault, or the schools' fault that many school environments are suffering from bullying, violence, poor student performance, and isolated students, but it is our opportunity to try to fix it. Developing Emotional Intelligence is about being able to see the possibilities that exist in front of us. Change Management is about changing our actions. Innovative Fundamentals is about connecting Emotional Intelligence and Change Management so we can connect our thoughts with our actions to make the right changes and achieve what we are truly capable of achieving.

EXERCISES

Who are the teachers who had the most impact on my life?

___

Have I made them aware of how they impacted my life?

___

Professional teachers teach our children in the classroom. Outside of the classroom, our children learn from the people in their environment. Who are you teaching? Who is looking at your habits and learning them as their own? If we know that our habits directly affect the quality of our life and the lives of those around us, then it makes sense that we would want to develop the habits we hope our kids will have.

What lessons from this book do I wish I would have learned as a child?

___

Are these skills being taught in the schools where I live?

___

A FINAL NOTE

The ability to change is more than just creating change.... It's hope, possibilities, and the ability to live with purpose and intention. It is about having the confidence, courage, and grace to create the change we want to see. Every great movement starts with a single thought from a courageous person who dares to see things a little differently. Because you chose to read this book, you are someone willing to see things differently, so you are that courageous person.

I hope this book helps you feel confident that you can create whatever comes next. Remember, you already know what you don't know...you just aren't aware of it yet. Take time to get to know yourself; I guarantee you will never meet a more important person. Whatever title you have, you are a leader. Lead yourself and others with confidence, courage, and grace. You are the most important organization you will ever work for. You are an authentic leader.

I hope this book inspires you to live your life with possibilities, and that, in turn, you will use it to inspire others to achieve their possibilities.

Think of the possibilities!

APPENDIX TOOLS

Having the right tools for the job is important. The tool grid below is a short list of the many tools you can use to create successful change and when to use them. Some of the tools were covered in the chapters and can be used for multiple steps in creating change. The Xs indicate the steps the tools can be used for. There is a description for all of the tools below.

	X = TOOL CAN BE USED FOR THESE STEPS				
	Self-Awareness Social-Awareness			Self-Management Relationship-Management	
Tools	**STEP 1** Define the Problem/ Possibility	**STEP 2** Where am I now?	**STEP 3** Where do I want to be?	**STEP 4** How do I get there?	**STEP 5** How do I stay there?
Winning Dance	X	X	X	X	X
Brain Hugs	X	X	X	X	X
5 S Technique	X	X	X	X	X
5 Whys	X	X	X	X	X
Brainstorming	X	X	X		
Affinity Diagram	X	X	X		
SWOT Analysis	X	X	X		
Trend Analysis		X			
Spaghetti Diagram		X			
Process Mapping		X	X	X	
SMART Goal Setting			X		
PDSA				X	
Visual reminders; calendars, checklists					X

Winning Dance

Imagine yourself in your winning situation—even if you have no idea what you are winning at right now. Feel your winning moment like you have achieved a success (any success). Imagine what that moment will feel like. Feel the energy running through your body, pump your arms in the air, yell out loud, drop to your knees, cry tears of joy, jump in the air, and smile like you have never smiled before. Then imagine how good it will feel when others are smiling excitedly with you and for you. These thoughts keep us motivated during the tough times. Your purpose will become clearer and clearer as little successes lead to big successes. Dopamine levels will increase as you continue to envision your success, and your motivation will soar. Practice your winning dance daily and feel how good it feels.

Brain Hugs (Mindful Activities)

Mindful activities are activities designed to give the brain a hug. They allow us to pause our thoughts and get into the present moment. They help us create a different relationship with the voices in our heads. Meditation is the most widely used mindful activity. It has been shown to improve learning, memory, emotional regulation, and sense of self. Its main goal is to focus on one thought at a time. Hundreds of different ways exist to meditate. The simplest way is to focus on your breathing for two minutes and increase the time as you get better at it. When your mind wanders, pull it back to what you are focusing on—each time you do this, you are improving your concentration and your ability to be in the current moment.

Meditation is not for everyone, so there are many other ways to give your brain a hug—dancing, painting, taking a walk outside, playing with your kids (two-legged or four-legged), taking time to recognize what you are grateful for, laughing with your friends, working in the yard, yoga, and anything else that gives your brain a hug so it can refresh and reset with clear thoughts and intentions. See if you can give your brain at least one hug a day for two to fifteen minutes.

5S Technique

5S is a tool used in Lean Six Sigma and other process improvement methods. It is a method for organizing the areas where you work. You can organize your workspace, kitchen, garage, closet, and even your thoughts using the same 5S method.

Sort—Keep the items you use most often nearby and put things away that you don't use very often to reduce clutter. Practicing your self-awareness skills keeps your important thoughts readily available so you can access them easily. When we can keep our thoughts sorted, we can make sense of them in the same way that we can make sense of our desk when it is sorted.

Straighten—Establish designated spaces for the things you use often so you always know where to find them. Put fear, anger, sadness, and other negative feelings where they belong so you can understand where they are coming from.

Shine—Keep your environment and equipment ready for use at any time. If your clock needs a battery or your lamp needs a bulb, fix it. Get rid of old, broken habits that are holding you back from reaching your glory. Shine your thoughts up. Focus on what's going well and what you are grateful for.

Standardize—Put things back in their places after using them and create standard processes for routine actions. Create a standard practice of self-awareness to ensure your thoughts are in the right place.

Sustain—Maintain your improvement efforts by implementing ways to monitor your success.

5 Whys Technique

The 5 Whys technique is used in business to explore the cause-and-effect relationships of a particular problem. This technique helps get to the root cause of the problem by asking the key question, *why*, until you get down to the real reason the problem exists. The technique is quite simple. Each answer forms the basis of the next question. Five is the number of times needed to get to the root of the problem.

Problem statement: ______________________ is causing me stress, sadness, pain, or general unhappiness and is holding me back from achieving the best version of myself.

Why 1: Why is ______________________ happening?

- Answer: ____

Why 2: Why is this happening?

- Answer: ____

Why 3: Why is this happening?

- Answer: ____

Why 4: Why is this happening?

- Answer: ____

Why 5: Why is this happening?

- Answer: **Root of the problem:** ____________________________

Brainstorming

Brainstorming is a process for generating creative ideas and solutions. It is usually done in small groups and involves open discussion of thoughts and ideas. Individuals can use the same process to brainstorm their own thoughts and feelings. Keep in mind that we can't see our blind spots, but the people close to us can give us insight into those habits and tendencies. Once we practice brainstorming and get comfortable with it, we feel more comfortable seeking insight from others.

Rules for Brainstorming:

- Set a time limit for brainstorming.
- Let thoughts and ideas roll freely.
- Do not judge any ideas or thoughts.
- Record all brainstorming ideas and thoughts (sticky notes or paper).

When the brainstorming time has ended, capture the responses and evaluate the information you have recorded.

Affinity Diagram

An Affinity Diagram is a way to organize information gathered from brainstorming. It involves clustering thoughts and ideas into groups with others that are similar. Sorting thoughts and ideas brings clarity and focus and helps develop self-awareness. Cluster sticky notes into groups and determine how they fit into your organization. They will all most likely fit into one of your seven areas and your purpose, and give you some information about where you are and where you want to go.

SWOT Analysis – Strengths, Weaknesses, Opportunities, and Threats

A SWOT Analysis is a form of brainstorming used to identify the strengths, weaknesses, opportunities of, and threats to an organization. It involves evaluating and sorting brainstorming information into groups based on whether the information is seen as a strength, weakness, opportunity, or threat.

- **Strengths:** Characteristics of the organization that give it an advantage over others.
- **Weaknesses:** Characteristics of the organization that place it at a disadvantage relative to others.
- **Opportunities:** Elements in the environment that the organization could use to its advantage.
- **Threats:** Elements in the environment that could cause trouble for the organization.

Strong relations between strengths and opportunities can provide the perfect opportunity to find passion and purpose. Strong interactions between weaknesses and threats could be a potential warning or danger sign.

Trend Analysis

Trend analysis is collecting information and attempting to spot a pattern, or *trend*, in it. For example, I notice when I go to yoga, I feel calmer and more relaxed. I also notice when I go out with friends on Thursday night, I am often late to work on Friday. Anything can be trended: our weight, spending, mood. Do you ever stop to think when you are at your happiest, saddest, most frustrated, bored, or excited? What are you doing at that particular time? Recognizing our patterns is helpful for seeing our blind spots, which is where our good and bad habits live. Remember, recognizing the habits that make us successful is just as important as recognizing the ones that hold us back.

Spaghetti Diagram

A *spaghetti diagram* is a visual representation using a continuous flow line tracing the path of actions throughout a process. The continuous flow line enables us to identify redundancies in work flow and opportunities to evaluate what we are spending our time on and why.

Process Mapping

Process mapping is a visual depiction of the steps or actions of a process. By mapping out the individual steps of a process, we can better understand how the process really works. Which means that we can understand how our actions are coming together to create the processes of our daily lives and our processes at work too. Remember, thoughts create our actions, and actions put together create our processes, habits, and behaviors. If we want better results, we have to create different thoughts and actions. If we don't understand the steps in the process, then we don't understand the process either. If we don't understand the process, then we don't understand what we are doing with our time, money, and energy. You wouldn't change your tire in the dark, so why would you stay in the dark about changing the processes that are creating your destiny? Understanding the steps and why we do them sheds light on how the process really works. And by "works," I mean how it gets done and how the end results work at creating the outcomes we want. This tool is fantastic for creating more time, money, and energy by defining the things we value so that we can focus on them.

Once you understand the individual steps and have mapped them out, evaluate them in terms of the value they add, or don't add, to the end result you want to achieve. Remember, value doesn't just imply monetary value, although that might be a benefit of improving a process. Value is the benefits, both internal and external, that come as a result of the action. I enjoy spending time with my mother. I value my time with her as precious because I know it so limited. There is no monetary value in spending time with her. The value is in our connection and love for each other. I feel good when I am spending time with her. It makes me happy. What you value may be different from what others around you value because we all come from different experiences and beliefs. Understanding what we value helps us to create the actions to achieve and sustain it. You are worth it.

Use the three criteria below to find the value and the waste in the actions you take. From the way you spend your money to the way you spend your time and energy, eliminating the waste (the things you don't value) will create more resources to spend on the things you do value. Every action you make throughout the day is part of a bigger goal you are trying to achieve. Whether you are trying to create fifteen extra minutes of free time for yourself in the morning, figure out why you keep blowing your diet every day between 6 and 8 p.m., building more reliable processes at work, creating a savings account for retirement, or helping your kids with their math homework, if you don't know what you value and don't understand how a process works, you most likely won't understand how to improve it either.

Value Added: These steps or actions are necessary and add value to the process or end result. If we use the process of boiling water as an example, we could say that putting the water into some kind of a bowl, glass, or dish is necessary for this process and adds value. If we skip this step, we would not be able to boil our water and achieve the results we want. Think green light.

Non-Value Added and Necessary: These steps add no value but are necessary to complete the process. In our water boiling example, the waiting time does not bring any value to the process, but it is necessary to create boiling water and the results we want. Think yellow light.

Non-Value Added and Unnecessary: These steps add no value to the process or end result and are not required to complete the process. Let's say from our example that while you are waiting on the water to boil, you slip into the pantry and grab a handful of Mint Oreos to pass the time. Although the Oreos are very good, they do not add any value to the process or the end result and are not necessary. Think red light.

Removing the "waste" or things that add no value to what we are trying to achieve creates more time, energy, money, and other resources to do the things we want to do and need to do. It's about working smarter instead of harder to achieve your goals and dreams. You are worth it.

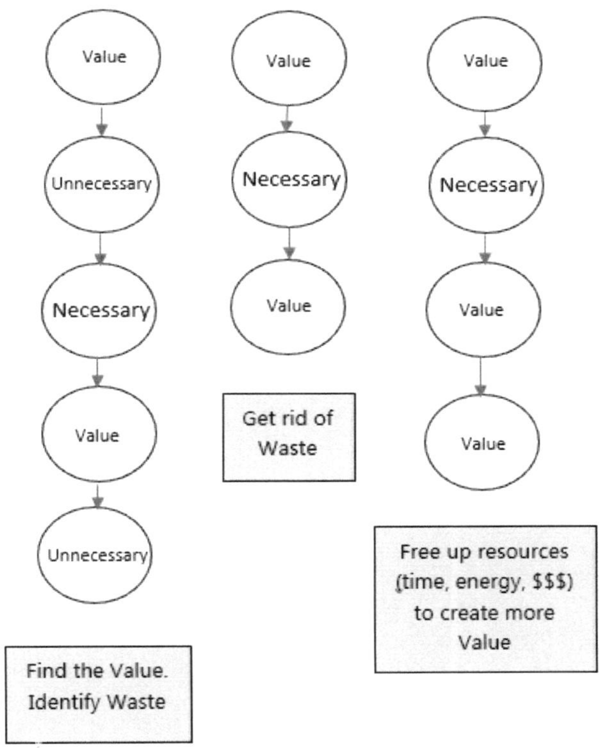

Smart Goal Setting

1. **S**pecific: Be specific about what you are going to achieve.
2. **M**easurable: Determine how you will measure your progress.
3. **A**ligned: Align goals with your overall mission.
4. **R**ealistic: Set realistic and achievable goals.
5. **T**ime-based: Include a time frame for achieving goals.

PDSA

You got this! Plan it, Do it, Study it, and take actions to maintain it.

Plan: Develop a plan based on the information you have gathered from Steps 1-3.

Do: Implement the plan. If the project is large, a smaller pilot project can be easier to manage and study.

Study: Analyze the information and study the results of the project.

Act: Make changes as needed and put measures in place to support continued success. Initially, keeping up your new habits will require self-discipline, motivation, and commitment. Putting visual reminders, text reminders, and even sticky note reminders in place during the early stages of transformation will help you stay on track in reaching your goals until the habits set in and the new habits become more automatic and require less effort. You can use this extra effort on something else… anything you want. Think of the possibilities!

Additional Tools for Maintaining Success

Overcoming habits and maintaining positive changes can be difficult. Until new habits are formed, using visual reminders like calendars, checklists, sticky notes posted, apps, etc. can keep you tuned in and aware of your progress.

ABOUT THE AUTHOR

Toie Martin is a professional keynote speaker, an author, and a die-hard optimist, who calls Amarillo, Texas home. She believes the ability to create successful change is more than just creating change; it's hope, courage, innovation, and possibilities. Toie coined the term "Change Coach" to describe her style of coaching/consulting that focuses on understanding change and developing the skills we need to create it successfully in all areas of our lives and work. Toie graduated from Midwestern State University with a BS in Health and Fitness Management and a BS in Nursing. After several years in healthcare leadership, she earned her MBA from Texas Tech and went on to get Lean Six Sigma certified and work as a change management consultant in the US and UK. She has been studying change in people and organizations for over a decade and is passionate about sharing what she has learned in the hopes of helping others develop the skills and habits to create the changes they want to see.

ABOUT COACHING, CLASSES, AND WORKSHOPS

If you and/or your group believe your best is yet to come and you are ready to develop the mindset and skills of a champion change-master superhero, but you need a program that is practical, easy to learn and use, and robust in results, then Toie Martin's approach to change is for you. In fact, she created it just for you.

Stop letting change get the best of you. Let Toie Martin teach you her five-step, practical approach for creating what comes next. It will change the way you think about and approach change for the rest of your life. Feel confident you know how to create the change you want to see. Contact Toie to find out more about her one-on-one coaching, workshops, and classes.

ToieMartin.com

ToieMartin@InnovativeFundamentals.com

BOOK TOIE MARTIN TO SPEAK

"Nothing is impossible. The word itself says, 'I'm possible.'"

— Audrey Hepburn

Speaking of possibilities...when it comes to hiring a professional speaker who will inspire, motivate, and entertain your group, you will find no one more respected or successful—no one who will leave your audience or colleagues with a more renewed passion for life—than Toie Martin.

Whether your audience is 10 or 10,000, in North America or abroad, Toie Martin can deliver a customized message for your meeting or conference. Toie's "get real" approach to creating successful change and reaching possibilities is inspiring, delightful, and powerful for creating what comes next in our lives and our work. Toie is a storyteller who understands your audience doesn't want to be "taught" anything, but rather, is interested in hearing stories of inspiration, achievement, and real-life people striving to live with possibilities.

As a result, Toie Martin's speaking philosophy is to entertain with humor, inspire with stories, and empower with knowledge and tools to create what comes next with confidence, courage, and grace. If you are looking for a memorable speaker who will leave your audience wanting more, book Toie Martin today! She believes the ability to create change is much more than just creating change; it is how we see the possibilities in front of us and achieve what we are truly capable of achieving.

To see a highlight video of Toie Martin, find out whether she is available for your next event, and contact her, visit her website. Think of the possibilities!

ToieMartin.com